Rhode Islanders Record the Revolution

Rhode Island Revolutionary Heritage Series
No. 4

Rhode Islanders Record the Revolution:

The Journals of

William Humphrey and Zuriel Waterman

Introduced and Edited
by
Nathaniel N. Shipton and David Swain

Rhode Island Publications Society
Providence, 1984

RHODE ISLAND PUBLICATIONS SOCIETY

Copyright © Rhode Island Publications Society 1984
All rights reserved
Printed in the U.S.A.
Library of Congress Catalog Number: 78-68840
ISBN: 0-917012-03-8

CONTENTS

FOREWORD

In the fall of 1775 Colonel Benedict Arnold led a major expedition of American troops in an invasion of Canada to seize British holdings there. After a grueling march through northern Maine and southern Quebec province, the Americans launched an assault on Quebec City on New Year's Eve. The attack was a disaster. Among those taken prisoner by the British was William Humphrey, a young officer who had previously served with James Mitchell Varnum's Rhode Island regiment. From the journal that Humphrey kept throughout the expedition there emerges a vivid picture of that ill-fated undertaking: the hardships of the march, the confusion of the attack on Quebec, and life as a prisoner of war two hundred years ago.

Zuriel Waterman, a physician from Pawtuxet, Rhode Island, was twenty-three years old in 1779 when he sailed as ship's surgeon aboard the famed sloop *Providence,* bound on a privateering voyage to Newfoundland. For Waterman this was the first of several such voyages, which over a period of some two years ranged with varying degrees of success along the east coast from Canada to the Caribbean. Waterman's meticulous daily record of these voyages offers an intriguing view of the sometimes dramatic, sometimes sordid day-to-day operations of American privateers as they pursued their own profits while coincidentally engaging in their new nation's struggle for independence.

This volume is the fourth in the Rhode Island Revolutionary Heritage Series, a compilation of Revolutionary-era writings by Rhode Islanders who were involved in the momentous events of that time. The series was inaugurated in 1974 when the Rhode Island Bicentennial Foundation issued as its first publication a biographical sketch and a collection of the political writings of the influen-

vii

tial Providence patriot Silas Downer. A treatise by Stephen Hopkins and the diary of a Rhode Island soldier named Jeremiah Greenman followed in the series, to which the present volume now adds the journals of William Humphrey and Zuriel Waterman. The Rhode Island Publications Society, continuing the work begun a decade ago by the Bicentennial Foundation, is pleased to make this volume available as part of our ongoing exposition of the history and heritage of our state.

Patrick T. Conley, Chairman
Rhode Island Publications Society

A JOURNAL

MADE IN THE YEAR
1775 AND 1776

BY WILLIAM HUMPHREY

Introduced and Edited

by

Nathaniel N. Shipton

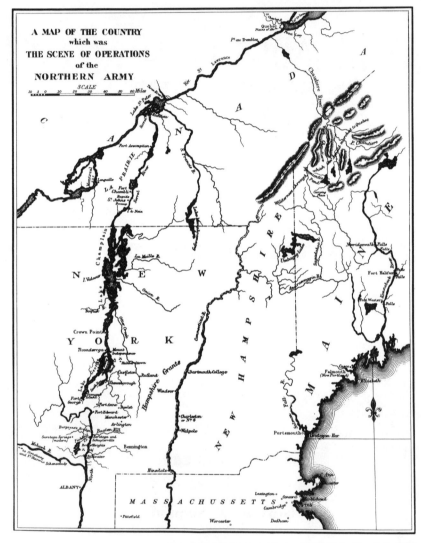

A MAP OF THE COUNTRY
which was
THE SCENE OF OPERATIONS
of the
NORTHERN ARMY

From George O. Trevelyan, *The American Revolution* (New York, 1907)

INTRODUCTION

Benedict Arnold's invasion of Canada began as a diversion for General Richard Montgomery's thrust down the Richelieu River from Isle aux Noix. Montgomery's first task was the capture of Montreal. Once achieved, this would open the St. Lawrence to Quebec, the fall of which would virtually destroy British influence in Canada.

However, at the time Arnold's ships were leaving Newburyport harbor for the Kennebec on September 19, 1775, Montgomery's army was stalled in a muddy siege twenty miles from Montreal at Fort St. John's. The little stockade fort defied the light six- and twelve-pound guns of Captain John Lamb's New York artillery company until November 3, when Montgomery had hoped to meet Arnold's force emerging from the wilderness near Quebec, three weeks' march away.

Meanwhile, on September 25 Arnold left Fort Western, opposite present-day Augusta, Maine, with two thousand men accompanied by some of their women. The principal guide for his legendary march was a journal made in 1761 by Captain John Montresor of the Royal Engineers. Montresor's route led up the Kennebec to Dead River, and from there to the Chaudiere, which joined the St. Lawrence just above Quebec. In all, the route covered 385 miles with numerous portages, some up to four miles in length.

Montresor had crossed these carrying places with canoes, not with 400-pound batteaux hastily built of green lumber, for Colburn's Kennebec shipyard had been allowed only fourteen days to complete Arnold's 200 batteaux. Splintered and leaking after the first carry, the craft became both cause and symbol of the marchers' agony.

Arnold's line of march was led by three rifle companies acting as light infantry. One company followed Captain William Hendricks of Pennsylvania, who died in the assault on Quebec. Captain Matthew Smith, also from

3

Pennsylvania, led a second rifle company. One hears little good about him. Francis Parkman, in the *History of the
Conspiracy of Pontiac* ... (Boston, 1851), pp. 441–13, ac-
cuses Smith of having led the massacre of peaceful Con-
estoga Indians in 1755. In keeping with his dubious past,
Smith apparently was so drunk that he missed participat-
ing in the assault on Quebec and probably died a
miserable death of smallpox during the Americans' spring
retreat.[1] Both captains deferred in most matters to the
famous Daniel Morgan, who brought a company of
Virginians.

The main body of twelve infantry companies marched
in two battalions under Colonels Christopher Greene and
Roger Enos. Greene was a highly regarded Rhode Islander
who later earned commendations for his defense of Fort
Mercer on October 3, 1777, and for his leadership of
Rhode Island's Negro troops in 1778. Three years later
he was murdered at Croton, New York, in bloody guerilla
fashion by DeLancey's Tories.

Colonel Enos led the last section. This Connecticut
native interpreted Arnold's October 24 order to send back
the sick so broadly that he took all 350 men of his division right back to Cambridge, leaving Arnold with less
than half of the remaining supplies. After acquittal by a
hasty court-martial, Enos resigned and eventually moved
to Vermont, where he became a man of importance in
state affairs.

Supplies were already short enough on other accounts.
While Mr. Colburn's leaky batteaux caused great spoil-
age, overturnings in fast water also took a toll. Yet, were
it not for Arnold's own miscalculations, these losses would
not have been critical. He had been "much deceived in
every account of our route, which is longer and has been
attended with a thousand difficulties I never apprehended. ..."[2] Arnold redeemed himself through energetic

---

1. Kenneth Roberts. ed., *March to Quebec* (New York, 1938), pp. 300–301n. However,
John Codman, in *Arnold's March to Quebec* (New York, 1902), p. 322, says Smith died
in Pennsylvania, July 21. 1794

2. Arnold to Washington, October 27, 1775, "Letters while on an expedition across
the State of Maine ...," *Maine Historical Society Collection,* I (1931), 366–67.

action, going ahead to the first settlement to send back food that arrived barely in time to save his starving army.

It was fortunate that Arnold's depleted and exhausted force met a quiescent Canadian populace. Most of the recently conquered French inhabitants saw no reason to fight for their old enemy, England. They reasoned, in peasant fashion, that it was better to sell these new invaders milk and loaves of bread for hard shillings. While this spirit of accommodation faded along with the Americans' prospects for success, 200 Canadians committed themselves wholeheartedly by joining a fighting regiment under Colonel James Livingston.

Livingston was a New Yorker who had settled in Canada after the French and Indian War. He and Major Jeremiah Dugan, "a former hair dresser in this place [Quebec],"[3] were two of a group of English Canadians who sought to align Canada with the rebelling colonies. Like many "old subjects" of the crown, they feared the same things colonists in Boston and Philadelphia did, especially the Quebec Act with its imagined consequences for Protestantism.

When Congress sent spies to Canada, Livingston and Dugan were undoubtedly among those giving assurances of popular support for an expedition. Seemingly, an American force would have to overcome only a few loyal troops and officials. All this appeared to be coming true. Montreal meekly surrendered to Montgomery on November 13, while Arnold landed unopposed at Wolfe's Cove below the Plains of Abraham.

However, Lt. Governor Cramahe refused all invitations to fight outside Quebec's walls. American attempts to deliver surrender demands were turned back by cannon shot, because such flags of truce were clearly attempts at spying. Governor Carleton's safe arrival after his escape from Montreal further stiffened the defenders. In the face of these developments, Arnold fell back to Point aux Trembles to await Montgomery.

---

3. Thomas Ainslie, "Journal of the most remarkable occurrences in the Province of Quebec from the Appearance of the Rebels in September 1775 until their Retreat on the Sixth of May," in Sheldon Cohen, ed., *Canada Preserved* (New York, 1968), p. 26.

The forces did not combine until December 2. After distributing supplies taken from British posts along the way, Montgomery set up headquarters at Menut's Tavern, a mile west of Quebec City. Colonel Lamb's guns were put into position as rapidly as possible, and again they proved too light to damage the walls. The gunners could only arch harassing shot into Quebec, which disturbed the garrison very little. Sniping by Morgan's riflemen, however, drew howls of anger. A customs official called them "worse than savages. . . . Lie in wait to shoot a sentry! A deed worthy of Yanky [sic] men of war."[4]

Smallpox, long a destroyer of colonial armies, soon spread from the city to the largely uninoculated Americans quartered among the inhabitants. Desertions,[5] raiding parties from town, and counterbattery fire from Carleton's heavy guns further depleted Montgomery's ranks. Finally, he had only 800 able troops when expiring enlistments forced him to make his disastrous New Year's Eve assault.

American losses numbered about 500, with General Montgomery among the 100 killed.[6] The survivors made a disorganized retreat amid rumors of a counterattack from the city, but Governor Carleton was busy digging out Americans still fighting in the Lower Town. Despite his own wound, Arnold assumed temporary command of the siege until orders could come from General David Wooster at Montreal.

This Connecticut veteran of Louisbourg arrived on April 1, 1776, fell off his horse, and went straight back to Montreal for treatment.[7] Massachusetts' General John

---

4. Ainslie, p. 27.

5. "6th [December] A woman of St. Roc gave information at Palace Gate that some of the Rebels lay drunk at her house. . . . This woman (of ill fame) . . . was told to let them know that they would be well treated if they came in; a little while after a man calling himself a cockney surrender'd himself at Palace Gate—at dusk three more came in." *Ibid.,* p. 26.

6. The best contemporary list is by Joseph Ware in "A Journal of a March from Cambridge on an Expedition against Quebec, in Col. Benedict Arnold's Detachment," September 13, 1775, in *New England Historical and Genealogical Register,* VI (1852), 133–36.

7. Wooster was killed leading reluctant militia against Tryon's Danbury Raid on April 27, 1777, the fight in which Arnold won his major generalship. Stanley M. Payellis, "David Wooster," *Dictionary of American Biography* (New York, 1938), XX, 525.

Thomas next took command on May 1. Seeing Carleton's reinforcements flow into Quebec from British ships in far greater numbers than Congress was sending to him, Thomas prudently fell back to Sorel. There the smallpox raging through the army killed him. Congress next sent General John Sullivan of New Hampshire to rally its shattered Northern Army. Resoundingly defeated in an attack on Three Rivers, Sullivan resumed the retreat, which did not stop until it reached Isle aux Noix.

Those who remained behind as prisoners at Quebec fared as badly as their retreating comrades. Particularly hard was the lot of the enlisted captives. Jammed thirty to a room only twelve feet square, the soldiers were cold, lousy, scorbutic, and pox-ridden. Each prisoner received a daily ration of a pound of bread, half a pound of pork, and a quarter pint of rice, with a weekly ration of six ounces of butter. Shortages caused by the siege later brought a general reduction to one pound of bread and one pound of beef. Some Quebec merchants donated a keg of porter with bread and cheese to soften the first days of captivity, but there was nothing to spare by spring.[8] Similarly, the shivering prisoners could not get enough firewood. None came in past the besiegers' lines, and the rebels systematically burned nearby houses that the garrison might tear down for fuel.

A prisoner in this situation had three chances to get out alive: he could enlist in the king's service, escape, or wait to be paroled. The quickest and surest way meant joining Colonel Allan McLean's Royal Highland Emigrants (H.M. 84th Regiment). Ninety-four English-born enlisted men signed up on January 8 to serve until June, under the threat of deportation to England for trial as traitors. After "six of the penitent rebels again repenting ... escaped over the wall behind the Artillery Barracks,"[9] the rest were disarmed and locked up again.

Other enlisted men who were as daring but valued their oaths more elected to try an escape that would have top-

---

8. John Joseph Henry, "Campaign against Quebec," in Roberts, pp. 384–85.
9. Ainslie, p. 50.

pled Quebec if it had succeeded. Using a hatchet smug-
gled in when they were taken prisoners, the men weak-
ened a door to the street. From there the escapers planned
to rush a nearby city gate, batter it down with its own cannon, and hold the gate long enough for Arnold's troops
to dash in. An agile prisoner actually slipped over the wall
in late March to warn Arnold that the attempt was immi-
nent, but an English deserter named John Hall, who had
joined the expedition in Cambridge, betrayed the whole
scheme. His former comrades were promptly put in irons
until May, when British reinforcements ended any threat
from outside.[10]

The officers made their attempt in April. A guard
agreed to join them with his musket, as well as supplying
clubs to subdue overly alert sentries. If all went well, the
escaping officers were to jump out of a garret window,
be marched to the city wall by their guard, who had the
password, and jump over into deep snow on the American
side. Unfortunately, Captain Simeon Thayer[11] went to
check the garret door one last time on April 26, only to
be seen by his jailer. Three officers were put in irons
aboard ships as punishment; the unfortunate guard was
sent to England and probably hanged.

By the time spring came to Canada, the prisoners' sole
hope lay in being paroled. Fortunately, Governor
Carleton's chains were meant to restrain rather than exact revenge for his charges' attempts. The governor saw
the rebels as children to be admonished and sent home.
Still, it was not until September 20 that Captain Thayer,
Lieutenant Humphrey, and just nine enlisted men from
the company's original eighty-seven landed in New
Jersey.[12]

---

10. "The time seems long, all in irons, though most of us pull them off at night.
I never lay but two nights with them on." James Melvin, "Journal of the Expedition
to Quebec in the year 1775," in Roberts, p. 448.

11. Thayer was formerly a peruke maker in Providence. Interrupting his career
to serve in the French and Indian War with Rogers' Rangers, he barely escaped the
massacre of prisoners at Fort William Henry in 1757. Thayer had an excellent military
career, retiring to a farm in 1781. Rhode Island Historical Society Manuscripts, VII,
48–55.

12. Simeon Thayer, "A Journal of the Indefatigable March of Col. Benedict Arnold . . . in the Years 1775 and 1776," *Rhode Island Historical Society Collections*, VI (1867),
1–104.

William Humphrey was twenty-four, a native of Swansea, Massachusetts, and had served in James Mitchell Varnum's Rhode Island regiment before going to Canada with Thayer. His release from parole enabled him to serve again in several Rhode Island regiments until discharged as a captain in 1783. In later years Humphrey held militia rank, was elected to the Rhode Island General Assembly from 1802 to 1812, and was a deacon in the Baptist Church. He died in 1832.

Humphrey apparently kept most of his journal as he went along, although the present copy is probably his transcription from what must have been a badly battered original. Both Captain Thayer and Captain Topham used it as a frame of reference to write their own accounts, making changes to reflect their own views and experiences. Such passing around of one another's journals accounted for fully one-half of the accounts listed by Kenneth Roberts in his *March to Quebec,* as is spelled out in detail by Justin H. Smith in *Arnold's March to Quebec* (New York, 1903), pp 24–55.

Past practice has been to publish these built-up accounts for their smoothness and greater scope. As a result of this, the basic journals have rarely been available to the general public. William Humphrey's story was finally printed in an extra number of *Magazine of History, Notes and Queries* (reprinted New York, 1931), vol 42, no. 2, but it was incompletely edited and is rarely seen today.

With the help of other journals, it is now possible to correct earlier misinterpretations and to fill in previously illegible words. Humphrey's habit of not punctuating his entries, his telegraphic form of writing, his erratic spelling, and his haphazard capitalization make an exact duplication of the original quite unreadable. The editor has therefore provided essential punctuation, corrected Humphrey's spelling, and put superfluous capitals into lower case. Additional words and phrases in brackets are intended to clarify otherwise unintelligible passages.

The editor is grateful to the Rhode Island Publications Society for the opportunity to publish William Humphrey's *Journal.* Particular thanks are due Albert T. Klyberg, Director of the Rhode Island Historical Society, who suggested the project and provided time to work on it. For the hours taken from domestic pursuits, the editor acknowledges the patience of his family. Both his wife, Sylvia, and his mother, Mrs. Dorothy B. Shipton, contributed helpful criticism, the latter drawing on forty years of checking historical manuscripts.

Nathaniel N. Shipton

Shirley Center, Massachusetts
June 1980

A JOURNAL MADE IN THE YEAR 1775 AND 1776

SEPTEMBER 9, 1775 Left Prospect Hill Fort in order to join the party going on a secret expedition under the command of Colonel Benedict Arnold, consisting of two battalions, one commanded [by] Lieutenant Colonel Enos and the other by Lieutenant Colonel Greene.

The first battalion consisted of:	Second battalion consisting of:
1 lt. col.	1 lt. col.
1 major	1 major
1 adjutant	1 adjutant
1 quartermaster	1 quartermaster
1 surgeon and mate	1 surgeon and mate for both battalions
Captain Smith's company	
Captain Hendricks' "	Captain Morgan's company
Captain Ward's "	Captain Williams' "
Captain Topham's "	Captain Hanchet's "
Captain McCobb's "	Captain Goodrich's "
Captain Hubbard's "	Captain Dearborn's "
Captain Thayer's "	Captain Scott's "

one chief colonel ⎱ for both
one chaplain ⎰ battalions

SEPTEMBER 11 AND 12 Remained in Cambridge in order to fill each company up to 84 effective men, and getting all things in order to march.

SEPTEMBER 13 This day our battalion proceeded on the way to Newburyport; marched as far as Beverly; stayed there this night.

SEPTEMBER 14 This day set out for Malden and lodged there.

SEPTEMBER 15 This day set out for the above said port,

11

where we came to about sunset and quartered our men in the Presbyterian meeting house.

SEPTEMBER 16   This day came at the said port all the battalion; we still remained in the said meeting house.

SEPTEMBER 17   This day we paraded our men and went to meeting. Then we were ordered to hold ourselves in readiness to embark at a moment's warning on 11 small vessels that lay ready to receive us on board.

SEPTEMBER 18   This day received orders for embarking, which we did about sundown; we was plagued to keep our men on board, for which purpose we set a guard to keep them on board.

SEPTEMBER 19   This day about 9 o'clock the whole fleet set sail for Kennebec with the wind WSW; we beat down over the bar; stood off until Col. Arnold came off and went on board the *Broad Bay,* schooner; the *Swallow,* sloop, run on a rock and stuck fast, and her men were put on board the other vessels; at 2 o'clock received signal for sailing and run down along the shore; gave the signal for heaving to off shore under our jib and mainsail.

SEPTEMBER 20   This day about daybreak spied the mouth of the River Kennebec; stood in for it; got into the mouth and came to anchor; stayed all day waiting for the fleet; they all came up but two, the *Conway* and *Abigail,* sloops.

SEPTEMBER 21   This day stood up the river, but the above said sloops did not come up; come to the head of Sheepscot River; saw the above said sloops, who went into Sheepscot River, which we thought was lost, which he was very glad to hear they was not.

SEPTEMBER 22   This day went on shore to Col. Arnold at Capt. Colburn's.[1] Then there was drafted 100 men to

---

1. Major Reuben Colburn of Gardiner, Maine. He commanded the carpenters on the march and returned with Colonel Enos. Justin H. Smith, *Arnold's March from Cambridge to Quebec* (New York, 1903), p. 76.

carry our boats to Fort Western; got all things in readiness for proceeding to the above said fort.

SEPTEMBER 23   This day we proceeded to Fort Western; this is a place of no great strength, whatever it might be in the first place; it has two small blockhouses and two large ones. It was built for a defense against the French and Indians.

SEPTEMBER 24   This day we were busied in getting our men up and provisions from Gardiner town; last night we had a man killed by a villain who snapped his gun at Capt. Topham and flashed at Capt. Thayer and then fired into the house and killed the man:[2] the suspected person was taken up about 8 miles from Fort Western and secured, but he was not the man.

SEPTEMBER 25   This day the murderer was taken up and tried by a general court martial and condemned to die; this afternoon an advance guard was gone forward consisting of 4 batteaux; yesterday the three rifle companies set off for Quebec, our designed expedition; received orders for our company to be ready to march at minute's warning.

SEPTEMBER 26   This day we set forward on our march; the above said murderer, viz., James McCormick, was to be hanged between the hours of 2 and 3 o'clock P.M.;[3] the river here is very rapid and difficult.

SEPTEMBER 27   This day we set forward for Fort Halifax, where I came to about 3 o'clock; this fort is much like that of Fort Western; the river is very rapid and rocky here; proceeded to the foot of the falls; here is a carrying place, the first we have come to; here we encamped on the west side of the river; we carried our boats and provisions over, which is about 80 rods.

SEPTEMBER 28   This day we proceeded about 3 miles

---

2. The man killed was Sergeant Reuben Bishop of Captain Williams' company. He was killed by James McCormick of Captain Goodrich's company. *Ibid.*, p. 319.

3. Actually he was sent back to Cambridge for final judgment by General Washington. *Ibid.*

through very rapid water; our people are obliged to wade more than half their time; it now begins to grow uncomfortable; here [are] a few scattered inhabitants.

SEPTEMBER 29   This day we proceeded on our march; we made large fires and refreshed ourselves; our people are in good spirits, but some keep lurking behind and by that means get lost from the party; at 12 o'clock set out again for Skowhegan falls; the stream is very swift, which makes it difficult, and our boats are leaky, which occasions our not getting along no faster; we have now got within 3 miles of the falls. Here we encamped; the water still continues to run very rapid.

SEPTEMBER 30   This day proceeded toward the aforesaid falls through rapid water; here is the second carrying place; we found that the course of the river differed from the draught that we had seen. I carried my batteau across the island and encamped on the main; on the west side of the river here is a new mill erected and the worst [con]structed I ever saw; the people call this place Canaan, a Canaan indeed, for here is as good land as I ever saw; the timber is large; here is pine, oak, and hemlock; last night it froze so hard as to freeze our wet clothes that we did not lie upon, and ice was as thick as window glass on the water that stood in a pail; the land is, I think, very fine and will produce very fine grain of any kind in an abundance; the people here are very courteous and strictly adhered to [the] cause of liberty, but they ask a prodigious price for their produce; their provision is chiefly poultry and moose and deer meat, salted and dried; here they catch in great plenty salmon; the cataracts are not so high nor so rapid as those at the forts, but being very narrow, which occasions the water below them to run very swift, here the carrying is difficult. Because the land is high, we had to carry our boats, provision, and baggage; this place is almost perpendicular (speaking in a comparative manner); our men are as yet in very good spirits, considering they have to wade about half the way, and they are very healthy, and if in their boats, they had as good be out, they're so very badly made; had they built them as ought to have done, they would have been much better. I hope that those infamous villains who, to satisfy their avaricious tempers and fill their own private concerns with the spoils of their country, [built the boats] may suffer like those of their countrymen that are obliged to make use of their boats, an invention of the infernal spirits, made for the destruction of the men that use them, for the boats are so bad that the men must be in the water whether in or out of them. This is the second carryng place.

OCTOBER 1　This day we proceeded on our march; got about 7 miles; made a stop for about an hour and set out again toward Norridgewock; came to the falls about 12 o'clock and encamped on the west side of the river.

OCTOBER 2　This day I had the curiosity to see an altar made by the Indians; here was also the remains of an old mass house where the Indians paid their devotion; here is buried their friar with the remains of a cross on the grave, which is the custom of the Roman Catholics; the friar's name is Francisco,[4] who about forty years ago was killed in an engagement when at this time the provincial troops killed and drove the Indians from hence; this place was famous in former days for being the Indians' headquarters. Here we was busied in repairing our boats and carrying our provision across; this carrying place is about a mile and a quarter; here we had sleds to help us over; here is the last inhabitants until you go unto Sartigan. Here Col. Arnold came up and stayed encamped on the west side of the river; this is the third carrying place.

OCTOBER 3　This day overhauled our bread and found it to be very much damaged; here we stayed all this day; got our batteaux and provisions across.

---

4. His real name was Sebastien Râle. He was the leader of bloody raids against New England and was killed in 1724.

OCTOBER 4   This day we came to the mouth of the Seven-mile Streams and encamped on a point of land.

OCTOBER 5   This day we proceeded on our march and came to the falls called Caratunk or the Devil's Falls; these fall about sixteen feet; the carrying place is about 8 rods and very difficult, over the rocks every inch of the way; we encamped on the west side of the river; the ice is on the river; the fourth carrying place.

OCTOBER 6   This day carried our boats across and proceeded on our way to the great carrying place; went about seven [miles] and came to seven islands fairly encompassed by the water; they lay on east side of the river; now we began to see the mountains that lay ahead; these appeared dismal in our sight, thinking we had them to cross; here I shall observe that we had no pilot.

OCTOBER 7   This day we proceeded on our way to the above said carrying; the land is low and full of very fine grass, but on the edge of the river it appears to be overflowed in the spring; it begins to be mountainous and less fertile; here I traveled by land till I came to above said carrying place, traveling through swamps, over hills and mountains, crossing small rivers.

OCTOBER 8   This day Lieutenant Church came back with his party that had been reconnoitering; returned back and gave accounts of the first carrying place being three miles and a quarter, then a pond. I shall give an account of them as I pass them. Encamped here and employed our men in clearing of the roads for carrying our boats; it rained very hard all this day, which occasioned our work not going on so fast as it would have been carried on if it was fair weather; we have been blessed with fair weather hitherto; at 3 o'clock all our battalion came up, but we remained; here the 3 rifle companies were helping to clear the roads; they had killed a moose. The skin appeared to be as big as that of an ox that would weigh 600 wt. This is the same species as that of the reindeer and would be of the same service to the inhabitants as

the reindeer is to the Laplanders and the upper Nor-
wegians; there is a vast number in this place so that we
can scarcely travel 50 yards without meeting with their
tracks. Their meat is very good and refreshing to our
men; we encamped here.

OCTOBER 9   This day detached two subalterns and 86
rank and file to clear the road to the first pond; the rest
of our men were employed in getting our pork on sticks[5]
and carrying our boats across to the first pond; the carrying place is 4 miles and ¼; the weather is fair but exceeding fresh; here came up two companies of the other
battalion; in this pond is very fine trout, of which we
caught a great number. [This is] the 5th carrying.

OCTOBER 10   This day we were employed in getting our
men across the pond; this carrying place is about half
a mile; then proceeded to the second pond; this is the
sixth carrying place.

OCTOBER 11   This day came to 7th carrying place, which
is about 4 miles ¼, and came to the rivulet that leads
into the Dead River, so called, but when they gave name
to it, they missed it very much, for the current runs very
swift in this river.

OCTOBER 12   This day we had a very fine prospect of a
high mountain which bore from us SSW, being 15
miles. Round this pond the land is boggy and wet; here
is [such] boggy ground that we carry our boat over that
every step [is] half leg high [in water] for a mile, and
to add to difficulty, we had to wade through all the
length of the bog; here is, at the foot of the bog, the
creek that leads into the Dead River at the east of the
mountain.

OCTOBER 13   This day proceeded on our march about 3
miles and encamped.

OCTOBER 14   This day proceeded on our way, not going

---

5. It would be easier to carry this way than by the barrel.

more than ten miles because of the current's running so swift and the shore so bold that our poles will not reach bottom in many places, so that we are obliged to haul our boats along by the bushes that hang over the water.

OCTOBER 15   This day we dispatched 2 Indians and [a] white man to Quebec with letters to a gentleman there, and we expect them to return in 10 or 12 days. Here we waited some time for a company that was in our rear to come up; employed in cleaning our arms; took another observation of the mountain, and it bore WSW; the river runs NW by W; thick weather and calm with some rain but not very cold; the land is fertile.

OCTOBER 16   This day, being very short of provision and brought to one-half pint of flour per man and waiting until 9 o'clock for the rifle companies in order to get some supplies, they not coming up, we proceeded on our way; came to an Indian hut where one Sataness lived, as big a rogue as ever existed under heaven; still proceeded on our way; march about 4 miles and encamped, and Col. Arnold came up in the evening at about 8 o'clock, and hearing of our wants of bread, ordered 4 batteaux with 32 men of each division to return to the rear for a supply provision in the morning; here our company had not five or 6 lb. of flour to 50 men; I was sent back with this detachment with a great deal of reluctance.

OCTOBER 17   This day we detached 12 batteaux with 96 men, officers included, who went on the above said occasion.

OCTOBER 18   This day employed in making and filling cartridges; took another observation of the mountain and found it bore SE by E, six miles; the river runs WNW and runs up more to the north; 'tis fair weather; here we tarried till the second division, commanded by Major Meigs,[6] came up and halted.

6. Major Return J. Meigs (1740–1823) of Middletown, Conn. He led four companies, was captured in the assault, and later took part in Wayne's storming of Stony Point. Smith, p. 265.

OCTOBER 19 This day it rained very steady until 3 o'clock in the afternoon, when Major Meigs with his division proceeded on their march toward the Chaudiere River. I should make some remarks on the prospect of the mountain and river, but that the work of Nature may at one place please the eye and displease at another, I leave it to higher geniuses and better judges to take notice of these and content myself entirely to our march. Our detachment[7] were, as long as liquor lasted, a most ungovernable crew; we expect our supply of provision, as officers and men are very desirous to get forward.

OCTOBER 20 This day it rained very hard; our boats not having got up, we packed up our cartridges in casks in order to be ready for an immediate embarkation; here stayed this night, it being the third day that we have been obliged to lay by for a supply of provision.

OCTOBER 21 This day it rained very hard and was almost as heavy a storm as I ever was sensible of; Colonel Enos came up with us at about 11 o'clock and expected to have found Col. Arnold, but on his not finding him, returned back; drove up his rear. In the afternoon there came up one of Capt. Williams'[8] sergeants with that company. Major Bigelow,[9] who had been down with our boats for provision, returned with only two barrels of flour; we are very short of provision, and there is no probability of getting any more until we get to Sartigan; now we have no other view than either to proceed to Canada or to retreat; we concluded to send all those back who were not able to do actual duty; this night the river has rose to a high degree, better than two feet and half, which occasions the current to run very swift; our encampment grew

---

7. The following lines were written, then scratched out at this point: "consists of the worst Americans and almost one-half of deserters or nit wits of the British army and navy."

8. Thomas Williams soon voted to return home with Enos. His further career is unknown.

9. Major Timothy Bigelow (1740–1790) of Worcester, Mass. He later became colonel of the 15th Massachusetts Regiment. Smith, p. 283.

very uncomfortable, especially for those who had no tents and not being used to soldiers' fare.

OCTOBER 22   This day the storm abated; the freshet has rose six feet perpendicular and runs down exceedingly. The sun arose with a little rain, but the weather grew fair; we began to embark on board of our boats, proceeding toward the Chaudiere; after going about 6 miles against the freshet, which ran at least 5 miles an hour, came to a carrying place which was overflowed, [so] that our boats went over through the woods where it was cut out for carrying our boats across; went about 50 rods and encamped.

OCTOBER 23   This day at 3 o'clock proceeded against the freshet, which is as full as ever, and this is paying for delay of time; went about 2 miles along and crossed another and half a mile further crossed another and went about 7 miles and came to another and expected to be within 8 miles of the great carrying place and encamped.

OCTOBER 24   This day received accounts of its being 25 miles to the height of land, and we are almost destitute of provision, being brought to half pint of flour per man and having no more to deliver out, it being the last we had; it snowed this evening and continued part of the night.

OCTOBER 25   This day we stayed for Col. Greene, who is gone forward to hear what we must do for provision. We are absolutely in a dangerous situation; however, I hope for the best, but if we receive no supplies from the French side, we shall be poorly off; this day there was a subaltern and 48 men of the sick went back with three batteaux; the river is narrow and exceeding swift; the going by land is very bad; the men is very much disheartened and desirous to return; however, if their bellies were full, I believe they would rather go forward; we are out and must go on. Col. Arnold has sent Capt.

Hanchet[10] with a party, the number I do not know, to purchase of the French if possible and to clear the roads; in the afternoon went about 3 miles and encamped to wait for our boats; here Col. Greene, Capt. Topham,[11] and Thayer stayed by desire of Col. Enos in order to hold a council of war, in which it was determined that Col. Enos should not go back.

OCTOBER 26   This day we proceeded over 3 carrying places, 2 small ones and one about ½ a mile and through a pond that is about ¼ of a mile and a carrying place as much more and came to another pond and encamped.

OCTOBER 27   This day, after a cold and frosty night, proceeded through this pond and came to another carrying place, this is the 15th carrying place and is three-quarters of a mile, and then came to another pond and encamped.

OCTOBER 28   This day we proceeded across the 16th carrying place and came to another small pond, to a carry place and then to [a] pond, to a carrying place, then to a pond and then came to the height of land, to another carrying place, four miles and a quarter; carried across and came to a small rivulet which leads into the great Megantic Lake, or otherwise the Chaudiere pond, which is 12 miles in length and 6 in breadth. Here we left our boats in our division, but one to take the sick in if any there should be; at 4 o'clock an express came from Col. Arnold with intelligence that the French was glad to receive us and that they would supply us with provision, glad tidings to people that are brought to one-half pint of flour and but very little meat; today was delivered out all the meat we had in

10. Oliver Hanchet (1741–1816) of Suffield, Conn. He was paroled in 1776 and left the service. Simeon Thayer, "A Journal of the indefatigable march of Col. Benedict Arnold ... in the years 1775 and 1776," *Rhode Island Historical Society Collections*, VI (1867), 82.

11. John Topham (1748–1793) of Newport, R.I. He was discharged with the rank of colonel and served in the Rhode Island General Assembly until 1792. *Ibid.*, p. 80.

our battalion, which turned out 5 pints of flour and 2 oz. of meat per man. An express passed us to go to His Excellency Genl. Washington; a pilot[12] was sent us to lead us the right way through the woods; two companies of the musketry are gone forward, but the 3 rifle companies stayed with us; this is the 19th carrying place.

OCTOBER 29   This day we proceeded in the front on our way to Sartigan; the traveling is very bad so that almost every step we sink in half leg high, but we have encouragement by our pilot that it is better ahead. Lost one man belonging to Capt. Topham's company, viz., Samuel Nichols, who must inevitably perish; we now find the pilot knows the way no better than we do; we traveled about 5 miles and encamped.

OCTOBER 30   This day we proceeded through a swamp 6 miles and more in frozen water and mud half leg high; got into an alder swamp; steering E southerly; came to a small river which we forded; the water was middle high and very cold; this river is about 3 rods wide, from whence we proceeded to a hill and then shaped our course N ½ W and came to another river that we crossed on a log; here several of our men had the luck to fall in; I must confess that I began to be concerned about our situation, having only 4 days provision in this wilderness, where there was no signs of any human being, but a swampy thicket of wood made only for an asylum of wild beasts. At ½ after 4, going about 13 miles and very bad traveling, came into a very fine grove of birch wood and, going about 2 miles and a half, found to our great satisfaction a path or track of human footsteps and greatly rejoiced; our men, who now begin to look pale upon their long march, and suffering both cold and hunger, encamped at the end of the grove.

---

12. The pilot was Lieutenant Isaac Hull of Connecticut. Arnold's orders read, "By no means keep the brook, which will carry into a swamp...." Order of October 27, 1775, printed in Kenneth Roberts, ed., *March to Quebec* (New York, 1938), p. 79.

OCTOBER 31   This day we proceeded 6 miles and then saw wrecks of some boats; went 6 miles further, not coming up with Col. Greene; here a man was drowned out of the boats; encamped.

NOVEMBER 1   This day we proceeded on our way; our people grew very much fatigued and begin to fall in the rear, being very much reduced with hunger and cold; I saw with astonishment a dog killed and [they] even eat his paunch guts and skin; went about 12 miles and encamped.

NOVEMBER 2   This day we proceeded on our way through much fatigue sixteen miles; it is an astonishing thing to see almost every man without any sustenance but cold water; this you must think is weakening rather than strengthening; here a boy returns and tells us that there was provision within 8 miles of us; I saw several, when they came to see the provision, shed tears, they were so much overjoyed at the sight of relief.

NOVEMBER 3   This day we proceeded on our way and met the provision, got refreshed, then set out again and passed by 3 pair of falls and went 1 mile and encamped.

NOVEMBER 4   This day we proceeded on and came to a river which we forded and came to the first house about 5 miles from the falls; got a good repast. We were well treated and paid well for it, which was but ordinary at the best.

NOVEMBER 5   This day we proceeded and came 5 miles to another house, where provision was made for the troops; we bought fowls and refreshed ourselves; the people are civil but very extravagant with what they have to sell.

NOVEMBER 6 AND 7   We proceeded to St. Mary's, about 15 miles from our last stage; provision was made for the troops; the minister[13] was kind and let us have all

13. Father Verreau. Smith, p. 248.

that he had to spare; this place is well settled and good
land along the river but poor back upon the mountains.

NOVEMBER 8   This day we proceeded on our way, and
Major Meigs came up and went on with 20 birch canoes
to carry through the woods in order to carry us across
the River St. Lawrence.

NOVEMBER 9   This day proceeded 6 miles through settle-
ments, then entered the woods, which is 9 miles; went
15 miles and stayed at St. Henri's parish at a house near
the chapel of the same name; there dined and set out
again to Point Levis, where we arrived at 8 o'clock;
found Col. Arnold and our volunteers all well and in
good spirits; this day the *Hunter*, sloop of war, sent her
boat to fetch some oars; we spied them and fired upon
them; they put off in confusion, and Mr. McKenzie,[14]
a midshipman, was taken and brought to headquarters;
he tried to swim off, but an Indian went in after him
and brought him out; he is strictly adhered to the old
doctrines of war, viz., not to [allow us to] discover their
weakness. He is but a youth at 15 years of age, a genteel,
well-behaved, soldierlike young man.

NOVEMBER 10   Remained here, busied in getting provisions and necessities for our men; got some wooden
canoes to assist us in getting across the [river]; Capt.
Topham with his company were detached to secure
them from the enemy, who then had a frigate, or rather
a sloop of war, that lay against them; the above said
sloop belonged to Simeon Pease of Rhode Island, and
James Frost of the above said colony was at this time
lieutenant of her, who came from the above said colony, captain of her.

NOVEMBER 11   This day Capt. Hanchet [went] with 6
smiths to make spears and hooks for ladders; Lt.

14. George McKenzie, probably the brother of Thomas McKenzie, who commanded
the *Hunter*. Smith, p. 456.

Savage,[15] with a number of carpenters, went, made ladders for scaling the walls of Quebec.

NOVEMBER 12   This day Capt. Hanchet returned.

NOVEMBER 13   This day continued fixing ladders for the above said purpose; received some favorable accounts from Genl. Montgomery; in the afternoon a council of war wherein it was resolved to cross the river this night. It was a calm, moonlit night and cold; at 3 o'clock in the morning the *Hunter's* boats rowed down; was hailed by our people, but bringing to, she was fired upon, and it was thought that some of the men were killed or wounded, for there was a d——l of a hollering in her.

NOVEMBER 14   This day a boat came to Wolfe's Cove with one carpenter and four men which was taken by Lieut. Webb;[16] they were unarmed and bound up the river for some timber which belonged to government that lay in the cove; carried the prisoners to headquarters; 1 of them is a Swiss man from whom we had some intelligence; the others were Canadians; the enemy sallied out and surprised one of our sentries; we immediately turned out our men and marched up within 80 rods of the wall and gave 3 huzzas and marched in such a manner that they could not discover of what number we consisted of; they fired some cannon at us but hurt nobody.

NOVEMBER 15   This day we was busied in getting our men in order and regulating guards and other duty; the French seem for the most part in our favor; there is some fellows keep about our camps whom we suspect but can hardly take them up without affronting the people; last night the English troops set fire to St. John's and burnt some part to the ground.

15. Abijah Savage (?–1825) of Middletown, Conn. He was discharged from Sherburne's Continental Regiment with the rank of colonel in 1781. Francis B. Heitman, *Historical Register of Officers of the Continental Army during the War of the Revolution* (Washington, D.C., 1914), p. 482.

16. Lieutenant James Webb of Newport, R.I. He was a captain in Sherburne's Continental Regiment in 1777, resigned from the army in 1780. *Ibid.,* p. 578.

NOVEMBER 16   This day we marched our men in order to take some livestock belonging to government; we posted nigh to St. John's but found none [but] some yearlings and an old cow and left a strong guard to cut off the communication with the city and returned.

NOVEMBER 17   This day relieved guards and took two gentlemen, capts. of the militia in Quebec, who had been out in the country to see what interest [they] could make among the inhabitants; this morning an express arrived from Brigadier Genl. Montgomery with some agreeable news.

NOVEMBER 18   This day, when our people were relieving guard at the nunnery, Sergeant Dixon[17] had his leg shot off by a 12-pound shot, and after having it cut off above where it was affected, he died very soon.

NOVEMBER 19   This day relieved guard as usual; sent boats across the river in the night and transported some men and flour; intelligence came from Quebec of their strength, which by the best accounts that we can get is about 8 or 900 men; we likewise received intelligence that they discovered our strength both in men and ammunition, which we were very scant, not having at this time more than 5 rounds per man, and it was said that they were preparing to sally out upon us with seven field pieces to cut off our retreat if possible, at which time there was a frigate went up the river, which made us suspect that the news was true; a council of war called and ordered that there should be three days' provision delivered out and to hold ourselves in readiness to march a moment's warning; about 3 o'clock set out for Pointe-aux-Trembles.

NOVEMBER 20   This day an express arrived from Genl. Montgomery with accounts that Genl. Carleton with his men had quitted Montreal to our people and [was]

---

17. Dixon was a rifleman "possessed of good estate" from West Hanover, Pa. Thayer, p. 20n.

bound to Quebec, which he is determined to hold at all events.

NOVEMBER 21   This day sent off an express to General Montgomery and sent a man over the river to stop the men that were left over on that side; it freezes so hard every night that the river has a thin crust on it; our men brought to distressed condition, being destitute of clothing and obliged to do hard duty; we [set] a number of men to make a number of moccasins and shoes, but the leather is poor so that shoes will not last long on the frozen ground.

NOVEMBER 22   This day our express that was sent from Major Caldwell's[18] returned with letters from General Montgomery; then we had 2 lieutenants and forty men to be placed at the ferry and bridge over [the] river which is between us and Quebec. A man belonging to Capt. Topham's company who we supposed to be dead came up with the forlorn news that he and one Olney Hart, who kept together for some time, both being sick and wading through the rivers, after they had been 6 days from the height of land, Olney Hart was seized with the cramp which continued on him 5 days, when by the violence of the disorder he was drawn out of all manner of shape and died; Burdeen and 5 of the rifle battalion left him dead, and passed by another dead man of the above said battalion and came up with a horse which got away from the man who had brought provisions to us; they shot him, and they stayed 3 or 4 days, and some more sick came up, and [by] these means he and 7 or 8 men escaped being starved to death, having for seven days nothing to subsist on but roots and black birch bark, boiled and drinked the water, in which there can be no great substance; they said they heard by one that came up that a man and his wife belonging to the battalion of the riflemen were

---

18. The Americans had a headquarters in a house owned by Major Henry Caldwell of the Royal Highland Emigrants Regiment; his rank often appears as colonel, because he served in an "advanced rank" (i.e., brevet rank). Ainslie, p. 99.

both dead and some others; to consider how the soldiers [were] lying in Cambridge and then to reflect of our fatiguing march, [it] seems astonishing how it was possible our men could go through it, and indeed, was one of the officers from Cambridge here now to review our men, he would really think one-half of them was fitter for the general hospital than the field, although they are now recruiting fast, and if we can once more get clothes for them instead of their rags, [and] good living, it would bring them up again; there is some who have received [a blow to] their constitution so that they will never be the same man again. This parish called Pointe-aux-Trembles but church St. Nicholas; today two of our volunteers set out on their way home.

NOVEMBER 23   This day Col. Arnold called a council of war to choose a committee to examine into the conduct of Col. Enos and his detachment returning home.

NOVEMBER 24   This day we was informed that 4 armed vessels was beating up from Quebec; a canoe was dispatched with sergeant and six men to carry intelligence to General Montgomery's party, which was coming down to join our party.

NOVEMBER 25   This day the *Hunter,* sloop of war, schooner, and brig heft in sight and came to off Pointe-aux-Trembles.

NOVEMBER 26   This day the aforementioned vessels hove up and stood up the river to obstruct Genl. Montgomery's party from coming down; 7 or 8 masters of vessel and some others, one who brought a proclamation of Genl. Carleton's; the sum of the above said proclamation is that every man that has not nor will not take up arms against America should quit the city and the district of Quebec in four days from the date of this proclamation or be taken up and treated as rebels, and that the sailors was taken and put into the barracks and treated as soldiers, etc.

NOVEMBER 27   This day our detachment was ordered to hold themselves in readiness to march at a moment's warning; Lt. Brown[19] and 18 men, 1 sergeant and corporal was detached last night on a secret [mission] and returned in the morning with 4 cows, 4 calves, 2 horses, and a calash which belonged to our enemy.

NOVEMBER 28   This day Capt. Goodrich,[20] with 2 subalterns, 4 sergeants, and 64 men, was detached and ordered up to meet Genl. Montgomery's advanced guard with ammunition and to watch the motion of the said vessels, Capt. Morgan with a like number to go before Quebec to watch their motion that way; Major Caldwell's house was burnt down in order to hinder our taking up quarters there as we had done before.

NOVEMBER 29   This day it snows very hard; Major Caldwell's clerk was made prisoner; he informs the intelligence that we had before.

NOVEMBER 30   This day continuing snow; the 3 armed vessels above mentioned came down the river with a breeze SW, greatly to our satisfaction.

DECEMBER 1   This day received intelligence from General Montgomery of his being in the river with 5 vessels; there was fifteen barrels of powder and two boxes of lead.

DECEMBER 2   This day Capt. Ogden[21] arrived with stores of all kinds for the soldiers; Genl. Montgomery heft in sight, about 9 o'clock P.M. came into Pointe-aux-Trembles; we marched our men down to him; he received us with politeness; he is a gentle, polite man, tall and slender in his make, bald on the top of his head,

---

19. Lieutenant Samuel Brown (?–1828) of Acton, Mass. He was taken prisoner in the assault and paroled with the others. Heitman, p. 122.

20. Captain William Goodrich of Great Barrington, Mass. He served in Putnam's Brigade in 1777 and later in the Massachusetts militia. *Ibid.*, p. 252.

21. Matthias Ogden (?–1791) of New Jersey. He was wounded at Quebec, left the army in 1783 with brevet rank of brigadier general. *Ibid.*, p. 418.

resolute, mild, and of a fine temper and an excellent general.

DECEMBER 3   This day general orders was given out for distributing clothes for the soldiers; this happy news of our men, as they were almost destitute of clothes.

DECEMBER 4   This day finished delivering out the clothes and received orders for marching to visit Quebec once more.

DECRMBER 5   This day at 10 o'clock orders was issued for marching, and at 12 our men were mostly gone.

DECEMBER 6   This day fair and cold.

DECEMBER 7   This day two companies [to] Beauport to watch the motion of the enemy; Capt. Dugan and Capt. Smith took 6 men and a vessel loaded with provision and small stock and 382 dollars belonging to government.

DECEMBER 8   This day we were busied in regulating guards and quartering our men; brought two field pieces to Mr. Menut's Tavern.

DECEMBER 9   This day prepared for fortifying and drafted men for fatigue, 100 men, and 100 men to cover the mortars and 20 men for an advanced guard.

DECEMBER 10   This day they spied our battery; they fired upon it all day and hove some shells but to no effect.

DECEMBER 11   This day they fired very briskly but to no effect.

DECEMBER 12   This day we fired a few shot from our battery.

DECEMBER 13   This day we completed our men with 26 rounds a man of cartridges.

DECEMBER 14   This day they fired a ball through our breastwork which mortally wounded 2 men; 5 slightly wounded.

DECEMBER 15   This day opened our battery upon the garrison; fired brisk all day.

DECEMBER 16   This day there was a brisk fire kept up on both sides; we had one man killed; Col. Arnold was obliged to quit his quarters on the [account] of their firing so briskly upon it; a council of was was held wherein it was determined to storm the garrison at all events.

DECEMBER 17   This day returns was made of what arms our companies had.

DECEMBER 18   This day a general return was made by the adjutant for all the arms and ammunition wanting in our detachment.

DECEMBER 19   This day we were busied in delivering the arms and ammunition to our men.

DECEMBER 20   This day ditto.

DECEMBER 21   This day nothing happened extraordinary.

DECEMBER 22   This day nothing extraordinary.

DECEMBER 23   This day Adjutant Fehiger[22] received a letter from Montreal but no intelligence.

DECEMBER 24   This day busied in making cartridges and balls.

DECEMBER 25   This day orders were given for every captain of Col. Arnold's detachment to march their companies to Mr. Devine's,[23] and there to be reviewed by His Excellency General Montgomery.

DECEMBER 26   This day nothing happened extraordinary.

DECEMBER 27   This day stormy; the men was ordered

22. Major Christian Fehiger or Febiger (?–1796) of Copenhagen, Denmark. He served in the Virginia militia as a colonel after being exchanged from Quebec and was discharged brevet brigadier general in 1783. Heitman, p. 223.

23. Morgan's headquarters.

to hold themselves in readiness to the shortest notice; at about twelve at night, the army being divided according to the plan the general had laid, part of our detachment proceeded to the hill; the other part stayed to attack the lower town under the command of Col. Arnold, but it clearing up, it was thought prudent to defer storming the garrison until a favorable opportunity.

DECEMBER 28   This day some of our men took four men that refused to turn out and led them around with halters around their necks from place to place and treated them in such a manner as all such villains deserve after going through almost everything but death in the march from Cambridge to this place; the general issued in orders, to the satisfaction of the soldiers in general, of the pleasure that he took in seeing the men so expert and alert in turning out in order to storm the city of Quebec.

DECEMBER 29   This day was delivered out clothing to the men; there was a number of shells sent into the town; a file of men was sent to one Mr. Drummond's still house to fetch a man that stayed there who we suspected to give intelligence to the enemy; they found him and brought him off, and in bringing him off, one of our men was wounded; Capt. Dugan took up another who had for some time carried on a correspondence with our enemy.

DECEMBER 30   This day the enemy kept up a smart fire all day upon St. Roques but did little or no damage; this evening about 10 o'clock received orders that it was the general determination to storm the city of Quebec; then we ordered our men to get their arms in readiness for to go and storm; it was very dark and snowed; the plan for executing design is as follows: General Montgomery with the York troops to proceed around Cap Diamond to a place by the name of the Potash and make his attack there, Col. Livingston with a party of Canadians to make a false attack upon Cap Diamond and St. John's Gate, an advance party of 25 men to proceed to Drummond's wharf, Col. Arnold's detachment to attack the lower town; in the following orders, Capt. Morgan's company in the front; the front commanded by Col. Arnold and Lt. Col. Greene; next Capt. Lamb of artillery, one field piece; Capt. Dearborn,[24] Capt. Topham's, Capt. Thayer's company, Capt. Ward,[25] Major Bigelow in the center; Capt. Hendricks, Capt. Smith, Goodrich, and Hubbard,[26] and Major Meigs in the rear. We were to receive a signal by 3 skyrockets when to attack, but not observing them, we was about ½ hour too late; Capt. Dearborn's company, on the account of being quartered on the other side of [St.] Charles River and tide being high, not coming up, however, we proceeding without them, expecting them to drive up the rear, we forced and took the guard; captain [of the guard] was drunk and not able to stand on his legs without assistance, which I think a very scandalous action for any gentleman, more especially on guard; they fired very briskly upon us; we passed along the street, and they killed and wounded a number of our men; among the rest there was wounded Capt. Hubbard, who afterward died in the general hospital; after we had gained the first barrier, we rallied our men and tried to scale the second barrier, and notwithstanding their utmost efforts, we got some of our ladders up [but] was obliged to retreat, our guns being wet, as not one to ten would fire; then we was concluded to retreat, which we did to first barrier that we had took, and when we came there we found we could not retreat without losing all our men or at least the most of them; there was killed of our party Lieut. Humphreys[27] and Lt. Cooper,[28] together with Capt. Hendricks with a number of privates, and in General Montgomery's party there was killed the brave General Montgomery, his aide-de-

---

24. Henry Dearborn (1751–1829) of North Hampton, N.H. He kept a diary of the march and later became commander in chief of the United States Army.

25. Samuel Ward (1756–1829) of Westerly, R.I. He was a lieutenant colonel by war's end and became a merchant in New York. Smith, p. 284.

26. Jonas Hubbard of Worcester, Mass. *Ibid.*

27. John Humphreys of Virginia. He came with Morgan. Thayer, p. xv.

28. Samuel Cooper of Connecticut. Heitman, p. 170.

camp McPherson,[29] Capt. Cheesman,[30] and some privates. Col. Campbell[31] then took command and ordered them to retreat, so that the force of the garrison came upon us; Capt. Lamb among the rest was wounded; there was no possibility of our retreating.

DECEMBER 31   They promising us good quarters, we surrendered ourselves; Col. Arnold, being wounded in the front of the action, was carried off to the general hospital; thus after a long and tedious march, I have been unfortunate enough to become a prisoner; here you may [see] the power of fortune, being in danger of starving in the woods and in danger of drowning in the river, where some of our men did, yet fortune was kind enough to save me from either starving or drowning to bring me to this place to be made a prisoner, which I think to be no great favor; now you may see that in fortune there is nothing solid nor permanent in her greatest favors, for in the very moment of victory, we have the most to fear.

The officers killed and wounded attempting to storm Quebec:

Killed
General Richard Montgomery
Capt. Cheesman
Capt. Hendricks
Aide-de-camp McPherson
Lieut. Humphreys
Lieut. Cooper

Wounded
Capt. Hubbard, who died
Capt. Lamb
Adjutant Steele
Lieut. Tisdale

As to the private men, I can give no account of how many was killed or wounded, but let them [be] as many

---

29. Captain John McPherson of Delaware. Heitman, p. 375.
30. Captain Jacob Cheesman of New York. *Ibid.*, p. 152.
31. Lieutenant Colonel Donald Campbell of New York. He served until 1784. *Ibid.*, p. 141.

as there will, in my opinion they have died in a glorious cause, and every man [is] worthy of bearing the name of Englishman. I was carried off, after my resigning myself prisoner, to the main guard, where I dined in the afternoon; I among the others that was taken was carried to the seminary, where they provided for us straw beds, mattresses, and blankets, which made our lodging very comfortable.

JANUARY 1, 1776   Here I spent a very solitary New Year; I wish it lay in my power to make my confinement more agreeable; every thinking man must know that it cannot be very agreeable to any person to be in prison or to be a prisoner, etc.

JANUARY 2   This day, the third of my imprisonment, Major Meigs was allowed by Genl. Carleton to go out and get in our baggage and to return on Friday; here we were visited by some officers of the garrison; nothing more happened extraordinary this day.

JANUARY 3   This day, by the consent of the general, Doctor Bullen came and inoculated myself and fifteen of our officers; we were visited as before by the officers of the garrison.

JANUARY 4   Major Meigs returned with baggage, but as it happened, he did not get mine.

JANUARY 5   This day, we being separate, we had liberty to go see those officers that was not inoculated, for they had the smallpox before, which made our situation more agreeable.

[JANUARY 6—MAY 4 ?]   I have not lost myself by having had my pens and ink taken, from which all the rest shared the same fate; it was done by the general's orders, and by that means it is impossible for me to keep a journal as before; we were at this [time] in two different rooms, which made our situation somewhat agreeable, but alas, in the midst of our joy we were informed that we must all go into one room again; we endeavored to keep apart for some time, but on one

Mr. Hutchins' saying that there was a great number of our men on the outside of the garrison, in the hearing of one of the sentries, we was all put into one room and our situation made more disagreeable, some of us not entirely well and in a room not exceeding 30 feet square and our number 36; thus we remained, having every day more or less of the officers to see us, a field officer; after Capt. Lamb came from the hospital, which made 37 of us, the barrier was removed farther back, and we were allowed two small rooms for twelve men to sleep in, which was some help to us.

[MAY 5 ?]   This day was found by the officer of the guard some of our men cutting the door; Mr. Wachope, who had the command of the guard, abused Capt. Thayer very much; the officer is a man that speaks German and says he has been good many years in the service; if he has, I think he is a very rude and unpolite soldier as ever I met with. Capt. Thayer was sent on board of schooner, and the day following, Col. McLean, Major Caldwell, and several other officers came and took Capt. Lockwood[32] and Capt. Hanchet, who was sent on board the above said schooner, and all three of them in irons; thus we continued.

MAY 6   The night between the 5 and 6 of May we heard different guns fired down the river, and in the morning we saw a frigate coming up to Point Levis; she kept up a constant fire, and the garrison shot into the river to let them know that they were still in possession of the garrison; they then came up and saluted the garrison; about 10 o'clock there came up a 50-gun ship, Capt. Douglas[33] commander, and saluted, and with her came a sloop of 14 guns; in these there came some officers and soldiers; these men, with what was in the garrison, sallied out, and our men retreated with so much precipitation that they left their cannon stores and am-

32. Samuel Lockwood of Connecticut. He resigned from the service in 1779. Heitman, p. 355.
33. Captain Sir Charles Douglas. Ainslie, p. 104.

munition, yea, even the general's coat and dinner, behind them; in the evening a small sloop went down the river with pilots for the fleet that is expected up; one frigate and a sloop of war was ordered up the river to take some vessels from our people, which they took one sloop and a brig which our people had scuttled and left, but in a schooner was taken Lieut. McDougal and three men with thirteen barrels of powder; today Capts. Thayer, Lockwood, and Hanchet was brought back and relieved from irons, the schooner being bound up the river.

MAY 7   This day Brigade Major Le Maistre[34] came [to tell us that] General Carleton intended hereafter to use us with as much humanity as lay in his power and hoped that we would not make a bad use of it; had again the liberty of walking in the passage, of which we had been debarred from awhile; we were this afternoon visited by Lord Petersham and Major Carleton; he is genteel and polite and truly humane; Caldwell was expressing himself [with] his usual sneer that he had suffered much by our people, and Major Carleton reproved him in these words, "You should not say anything disagreeable to them in their situation, for we are all brothers." He said that there was a great number of Hessians and Hanoverians expected over to America.

MAY 8   This day with the remainder of the 29th Regiment and some of the artillery; we were visited by some of the officers enquiring for the troops that was taken at St. John's and other places.

MAY 9   This day we were visited by some officers of the 29th Regiment, a very polite gentleman especially, a lieutenant of the grenadiers; a small schooner came up the river; the garrison has men without daily to pick up what our men had left behind, such as [sick] and wounded; they have taken a vast number of papers, among others an orderly book; this evening was taken Lt. Randall, Stephen McDougal on board the schooner

---

34. Major Francis Le Maistre, 7th Regiment of Foot. *Ibid.*, p. 105.

Mary; he gave intelligence from our people, so that we are in hopes that it is not so bad as it was reported at first by the people of the garrison, but as it [is] I think it is bad enough.

MAY 10   This day two transports came up with provisions from Halifax, with a part of the 47th Regiment.

MAY 11   This day we were visited by Col. McLean and some other officers and were allowed to walk in the garden. Major Carleton visited us and said there was 55,000 men designed for America this summer and to be in three divisions; we desired him to obtain liberty from the general for our servant to cook for us, which he promised to do.

MAY 12   This day the answer was brought by himself that we might walk in the garden; some of our gentlemen went into the garden, but for my part, I did not; two transports arrived with troops.

MAY 13   We have this day been indulged more than common; we can walk up the stairs as often as we please; this day is the first time I have set my foot on the ground for the space of four months and thirteen days. A brig hove in sight and came to off Beauport on account of the tides not serving, but she was a transport.

MAY 14   This day about nine o'clock the 50-gun ship hoisted on her maintopgallant masthead a broad pendant, and she was saluted by all the ships in the harbor, and she fired 15 guns in answer to them; on the maintop masthead was hoisted a white pendant, and a pendant on her ensign staff; the garrison fired a salute of 15 guns in the afternoon; a frigate went down the river at night, and an armed schooner went up the river. Major Meigs went out with Doctor Maben to see about getting Mr. Monroe to supply us and returned again; he has obtained the general's promise of getting home upon his parole; we have had fair weather except a shower now and then; the tide here has risen from 19 to 22 feet with an easterly wind and from 16 to 19 with a westerly wind; the tide ebbs 7 hours and flows 5; the wind in the spring blows from eastward to the northward with showers of rain; the west and southward winds are in general fair and warm; it is very common for it to rain one-half hour and then clear up; they continue to lock us up every night as yet.

MAY 15   This day we were once more allowed to use our pens and inks. Major Meigs called upon by the general and promised in a few days to go off to Halifax on his way home on his parole; tonight two or three vessels came up the river; among them there came up a twenty-gun ship.

MAY 16   This day about 10 o'clock the *Hunter,* sloop of war, set sail for England with dispatches, in which went passengers Capt. Hambledon, Major Caldwell, and his family; we had liberty to write letters by Major Meigs provided that [we] wrote nothing concerning the garrison, which kept us all very busy, etc.

MAY 17   This day Lt. Born carried our letters to Col. McLean to examine; a small sloop came up; Major Meigs had liberty to walk the town till four o'clock. Laveris came and informed Capt. Dearborn that he had obtained liberty for him to go home on his parole and that he must get ready to go on board immediately. In the evening they took their leave of us and went on board the schooner *Magdalen.*

MAY 18   This day about 10 o'clock Major Meigs and Capt. Dearborn set sail for Halifax, and another small schooner went down.

MAY 19   This day saw a sloop of war come down, and the *Commodore;* about noon the *Surprise* came down the river and saluted and came to under the *Commodore*'s stern; a number of officers walking in the garden, among others one that was not above 15 years old. The drummers of the 29th Regiment are black men; the band wears red feathers in their hats and looks extraordinary neat.

MAY 20   This day thick weather and a little rain; wind from NNE; Doctor Maben visited Mr. Porterfield,[35] a sick volunteer, or rather encouraged him with hope of getting him leave for him to go home upon his parole in the first vessel bound to Halifax; we were allowed 2 small rooms for part to lodge in, which will make our lodging yet more agreeable than formerly used to be.

MAY 21   This day nothing extraordinary; the weather is cloudy and windy.

MAY 22   This day there went for Montreal three ships to try to drive our people out of the province of Quebec, in whom Genl. Carleton went; they fired a salute from the ships and from the garrison; we received intelligence from a Canadian that the 8th Regiment that lay at Fort Detroit and Fort Stanwix and Swagocha [?] with about 500 Indians came down within about 9 miles from Montreal at a place called Lachine, where they had an engagement, and it was said that they had killed and wounded 150 of our men, but I gave not much credit to it.

MAY 23   This day is clear and fair with the wind about WSW; we heard that the intelligence we had yesterday is uncertain; we was told by one Capt. McDougal that the inhabitants of Virginia has laid down their arms and that there is more of the inhabitants of that province on the behalf of government than there is on the part of America, which I think is mistaken.

MAY 24   This day is fair and clear with little or no wind; came up the river a small schooner with wood for the garrison; received intelligence that Montreal was taken.

MAY 25   This day is cloudy and some rain with the wind NE; no news worthy speaking of.

MAY 26   This day is fair and clear; Sunday.

---

35. Sergeant Charles Porterfield of Frederick County, Va. He became a colonel in the Virginia Line and died of wounds received in the Battle of Camden in 1780. Heitman, p. 448.

MAY 27   This day is fair and the wind at NE; this day between 40 and 50 ships of war and transport came up, and they were ordered to pass the city and go to Montreal as quick as possible.

MAY 28   This day is nothing remarkable.

MAY 29   This day a ship came up the river who fired a royal salute.

MAY 30   This day there came two ships up the river; this day is fair and clear.

MAY 31   This day is fair and clear; last night between the hours of twelve and one we heard the sentry hail three times and then fired; we looked out and saw the guard out in the garden searching to find the object that was fired at but could [not] find it; I believe it was nothing more than conceit of the sentry or a trap to have us more closely confined laid by some of our enemies, who would be glad to have our throats cut and would cut it if it lay in their power; 'tis certain that there is some who try to set them against us, that have more power in their hands than they have. One brig and ship came up the river and a schooner. The brig was full of soldiers, etc.

JUNE 1   This day came up four ships; they are constantly coming up; the intent of this army is, as far as I can learn, to offer terms of reconciliation and to hold the sword at the Americans' breast, saying, "Accept of this offer, or I'll cut your throat." This army consists of Britons, Scots, Irish, Hanoverians, Hessians, Germans, etc. O Britons, how are you fallen that you hire foreigners to cut your children's throats. 19 ships came up the river; we was visited by several of the Hessian officers, one colonel, his name Islitz; this evening 6 more ships came up.

JUNE 2   This day is cloudy, the wind NE; the ships are about to go up the river with the troops in order to give the provincials battle; they think to drive the

Americans as they please, but I think they will be deceived.

JUNE 3   This day is fair and clear; nothing new.

JUNE 4   This day is cloudy with some rain.

JUNE 5   This day is fair and warm with little or no wind; we hear that the Indians under the command of Capt. Foster took a number of the provincials prisoner and that the Indians made our people promise never to take up arms against the troops of Great Britain and that they should send as many of the king's troops back as there was of them in a way of exchange and keep several of the chief officers as hostage; for the rest there would [be] the hatchet at the head if they did not do as they said; they bored the ears of the prisoners so that they should know them again if they should catch them again, and then they are to be put to death by the savages.

JUNE 6   This day is cloudy and rains with little or no wind; about 6 o'clock it still continues to rain with some thunder; there is snow in Canada; we learn that His Excellency proffered to the men that if they would swear allegiance to the king, he would dismiss them, and they might go home; the men are almost naked and very lousy and have got the scurvy very bad, being in prison from the 31 of December without money or friends that could help them; they have not sworn as yet, but what they will do I cannot tell; by what I can learn, they must swear or die; if they remain in prison a great while longer, they must certain perish, as they can have no relief from home. No man knows what it is to be a prisoner till they are made prisoners.

JUNE 7   This day is cloudy with the wind at NW; snow is yet in this province; we petitioned to the general for liberty to go home on our parole, but we have had no answer as yet; we had an answer to our petition, which was that the general could not with propriety; we hear that the Eighth Regiment is taken by the provincials and that there is great disturbance in Great Britain, some on one side and some on the other side; we wrote another petition and sent to the general, but what will be the effect of it we do not know as yet; I had an opportunity to see some of our men who had taken the oath of allegiance; they look very pale, and some say that there is a considerable number of our people has lost the use of their limbs; I could wish that they was all at home; we have received an answer to our last petition, viz., that we might go home upon our parole; we have not seen the parole; we learn that General Thomas died of the smallpox at Montreal, etc.,

JUNE 8   This day is fair and clear.

JUNE 9   This day we hear that General Washington took at Bunker Hill 1,500 prisoners and the hill.

JUNE 10   This day is fair and clear with the wind NE; a brigantine came up.

JUNE 11   This day is fair and clear, little or no wind; a frigate come to sail about 6 o'clock and went down the river.

JUNE 12   This day fair and clear with the wind SW; this is the warmest day that I have seen in Canada.

JUNE 13   This day is fair, and the wind is NE, but nothing remarkable.

JUNE 14   This day is cloudy with the wind at NE; we hear that the provincials have killed 50 of the Hessian soldiers and sunk 3 of their ships that attempt to pass our works at Sorel; we hear that Philadelphia is besieged by the king's troops.

JUNE 15   This day is cloudy with a very heavy [wind] from the E; nothing new.

JUNE 16   This day is clear with the wind SW; we hear that there has been two skirmishes in which a considerable number has been slain at or near Sorel in this province, in which was taken Genl. Thompson[36] and his aide-de-camp and several others.

JUNE 17   This day is fair and clear with the wind SW, but nothing remarkable.

JUNE 18   This day is cloudy with some rain and the wind S and by E soon; 5 o'clock this day in the afternoon a merchant ship belonging to this place [arrived].

JUNE 19   This day is fair and clear with the wind at SW, but nothing remarkable.

JUNE 20   This day is cloudy and about 3 o'clock some rain and thunder, but nothing remarkable.

JUNE 21   This day is clear and calm; a ship came up last night; I believe that it is a merchant ship with dry goods.

JUNE 22   This day is clear and fair and calm and warm; about 6 o'clock in the afternoon there came up a thundershower and rained very hard, but no news worth speaking of.

JUNE 23   This day is clear and calm, Sunday; the provincials have burnt Fort Chambly and gone to St. John's, and it is said that there is from 300 to 7,000 of the provincials; this afternoon about 6 o'clock came up a shower.

JUNE 24   This day is fair and clear; at 6 o'clock it thundered with rain; a ship came down the river; we hear nothing extraordinary.

JUNE 25   This day is fair and clear; the honorable lieut. governor made a present to us of 10 gals. of rum; two vessels came down the river with prisoners taken at St. John's, Chambly, etc.

JUNE 26   This day is fair and clear and warm with the wind at NNE; we hear that the twelve united colonies has declared themselves an independent state and have

---

36. General William Thompson (?–1781) of Pennsylvania. He was captured in the fight at Three Rivers and exchanged on October 25, 1780. Heitman, p. 541.

sent to France for assistance and also that were received a large quantity of gunpowder and 6,000 stands of arms from them, etc.

JUNE 27   This day is fair and clear, the wind at about SW; two vessels came up the river and fired a salute and was answered by the *Commodore;* we are prohibited from going to the walls of the garden this afternoon, for what reason I can't tell; it is now very warm.

JUNE 28   This day is clear and warm with a little breeze of wind about SW; the ship *London* is gone down the river; we believe that it is gone to England; this afternoon a schooner sailed for the West Indies.

JUNE 29   This day is fair and clear, the wind about WSW.

JUNE 30   This day is fair and clear with the wind at E; last night two brigs came up the river; we can't tell where they are from as yet; at 3 o'clock there came up 1 brig, 2 schooners, 1 ship, etc.

JULY 1   This day is rain with thunder and sharp lightning.

JULY 2   This day is cloudy with the wind at E; we was prohibited going to the walls of the garden as usually, for what reason I can't tell.

JULY 3   This day is cloudy with some rain, the wind about SW; nothing has happened extraordinary.

JULY 4   This day is fair and clear, the wind at SW; we hear that General C[arleton] has sent for all the troops lying here in order to pass the Lakes Champlain; four officers of the provincials came and gave us an account of their being taken, viz., that they and four officers together with three soldiers went out in a boat to fish and then went across the river to a house to get some beer, the house not standing more than 2 rods from the shore; they unhappily had not their firearms with them, and secure as they thought from any danger, they heard the boy hollo and then, running out, see the occasion, expecting then there might be some of that cussed nation of Indians there; they had not made many steps before they was fired at by thirteen of the above said inhuman creatures; they then tried to get off the boat, but before they get her off, they killed one officer and wounded another; they then ran down upon them, when two found means to escape, but they took five officers alive, one of whom they tomahawked and then scalped the two officers, took off with those that they did not kill and, after tying them with their belts around their necks, set them before, making them to run as fast as they thought fit for the space of about one mile; they stopped and holloed,, as is common, for their comrades, paraded them to show the great feats that they had done, to their fellows; they set out again, and night coming on, they stopped and obliged them to lie on their backs, tied them fast so that they could not get up, and lying on the end of the belt, they went to sleep; the next day they set out again; one of the Indians cocked his gun and snapped at Wm. McFarland and then drew his own sword upon him; they then stripped them to their breeches of everything, then carried them to Montreal.

JULY 5 This day is rainy with the wind SSW; nothing has happened extraordinary.

JULY 6 This day is fair and clear with the wind at SW; last night we was locked up in our rooms, for what reason I can't tell; this morning there came up six vessels, three ships and two brigs and one snow; where they are from I can't tell, but I believe that they are provision vessels.

JULY 7 This day is fair and clear with the wind at about NW; this day several officers of the garrison came in our rooms looking around but did not say a word to one of us; we could not tell what was the matter, but there was some captain of the ships came in the garden where we was, and they said that it was said in the town that we was going to set seminary afire, but far be it from us; I believe that there is not a man here that would do it for his life; for my part, I would [not] do it for ever so much.

JULY 8   This day is fair and clear; we hear that there has been a general battle at New York, and some says that our people has killed and taken four or five thousand, and others say that the British troops have taken New York, and Virginia and Pennsylvania has gave up, and they shall soon be through the country, but we put no trust in what they say; we hear so many stories that we don't know what to believe ourselves.

JULY 9   This day is fair and clear, the wind at about W; this afternoon a sloop of war went down the river.

JULY 10   This day is fair and clear, the wind about W, etc.

JULY 11   This day is cloudy with some rain, the wind at E; this day there was a brig and sloop came up the river; we don't know where they are from, but we think that they are provision vessels.

JULY 12   This day is fair and clear with the wind at about west till about 3 o'clock and then began to rain and so continued till night; this day we hear that Major Meigs and Capt. Dearborn was exchanged by Admiral Howe, etc.

JULY 13   This day is fair and clear, the wind W; nothing remarkable.

JULY 14   This day is fair; at 4 o'clock came up a squall of wind; it shifted from W to E, from E to S in less than 10 minutes and a few drops of rain, etc.

JULY 15   This day is fair and clear, the wind about west, etc.

JULY 16   This day is cloudy and began to rain about 10 o'clock and rained till about sunset steady; the wind SW.

JULY 17   This day is cloudy, raw, cold with some rain; we hear that there has been a skirmish at a place called

Pointe-au-Fair; we hear that our people saw them in their boats and stove them to pieces, and killed and wounded and missing amounts to 400; about 4 o'clock brig went up the river, loaded I believe with provisions.

JULY 18   This day is fair and clear, the wind at west; we was locked close in our rooms last night; what is the occasion of it I can't tell; there was a ship of war came down the river from Sorel.

JULY 19   This day is fair and clear; the wind blows very hard at NE; the *Lizard*, thirty-six–gun ship of war, set sail for New York, as we hear; we hear that we are to be sent home as soon as the general comes from Montreal, which is expected every hour.

JULY 20   This day is fair and clear, etc.

JULY 21   This day is in morning cloudy and rains steady and so continued till night; nothing happened remarkable.

JULY 22   This day is fair and clear, the wind about west; this morning the *Bland*, 32-gun frigate, set sail and went down the river; some say she has gone to London, but I can't tell where she is gone; a brig and a sloop went away directly after down the river; this afternoon General Carleton came to town and was saluted by the garrison; they fired 15 guns; we was very glad to hear it, for we expect to hear whether we shall go home or not soon.

JULY 23   This day is fair and clear, the wind about SW; we hear nothing remarkable.

JULY 24   This day is showery, the wind at SW; there is 4 vessels gone down the river; two of them is ships, one brig, and a schooner, and one frigate came up the river.

JULY 25   This day is fair and clear, the wind about NW; nothing remarkable.

JULY 26   This day is fair and clear, the wind at NW; a large ship went down the river, and a brig came up the river; this day Capt. Foy came and told us that the general was very sorry to hear that we was not gone, but we should go very soon.

JULY 27   This is fair and clear, the wind at NW; this day a ship came up the river and another went down the river, etc.

JULY 28   This day is fair and clear; we hear that General Thompson shall go home with us.

JULY 29   This day is cloudy with some rain; General Carleton has, as we have been in such want of money, this day sent 100 pounds, which we expect to pay to some of the British officers that are in the colonies, prisoners, which we take it very kind of the general.

JULY 31 [No entry for July 30]   This day is fair and clear; General Thompson came to see us and said that Genl. Carleton desired him to call and let us know the terms that we should go home upon.

AUGUST 1   This day Genl. Thompson and several other gentlemen brought a copy of the parole, which we did not like, but Genl. Thompson said that he thought that Genl. Carleton would alter it, but if he don't, I believe we shall stay here 7 months longer.

AUGUST 2   This day is fair and clear; this day Genl. Carleton sent us word that he would leave out the word that we objected to, which word was that we should never take up arms against His Majesty; we chose to leave that word out, etc.

AUGUST 3   This day is fair and clear; this day the town major and Mr. Murray brought our parole, and we signed it [with] Genl. Thompson and several of the officers, etc.

AUGUST 4   This day is fair and clear; we hear that Genl. Washington refuses to exchange the men that was taken at the Cedars, and we hear that Genl. Carleton keeps sixteen men that came over the lake as flag.

AUGUST 5   This day we had orders to hold ourselves in readiness to embark at a minute's warning; we packed up our things and got ourselves in readiness to march.

AUGUST 6   This day is fair and clear; our men was called together to sign some papers; what it was I don't know; we received orders to embark tomorrow at nine o'clock.

AUGUST 7   This day about nine o'clock we embarked on board of the ship called by the name of *John Christopher;* about 10 o'clock 80 of our men came on board.

AUGUST 8   This day Capt. Foy and Mr. Murray came on board of the vessel to see how we was accommodated; Capt. Foy wished us well and said he hoped that when we met again we should be friends.

AUGUST 9   This day we lie waiting for the prisoners to come down the river and dividing stores out to the men, etc.

AUGUST 10   This day a brig with the prisoners came down the river, and about 11 o'clock the prisoners was brought on board of us, etc.

AUGUST 11   This day about 11 o'clock we hove up and went down below the town; the wind blew very hard at east; we came to an anchor, etc.

DIARY OF A DOCTOR–PRIVATEERSMAN

1779 TO 1781

BY ZURIEL WATERMAN

Introduced and Edited

by

David Swain

The swift-sailing Sloop H O P E.

On Thursday next will sail (commanded) plently fitted for a short Cruize of Fifty Days) the swift-sailing Privateer Sloop HOPE, mounting 10 Carriage Guns, CHRISTOPHER SMITH, Commander. All Gentlemen Seamen, and able-bodied Landsmen, who wish to try their Fortunes, may have an Opportunity, by applying at the Rendezvous, at Mr. Joshua Hacker's, or to the Commander on board, at Clark and Nightingale's Wharff.

From the *Providence Gazette and Country Journal*, August 4, 1781 (Rhode Island Historical Society, Rhi X3 1052)

INTRODUCTION

Life of Zuriel Waterman

Zuriel· Waterman was born at Pawtuxet, a section of present-day Cranston, Rhode Island, on January 20, 1756. His father, Christopher Waterman (1722–1758), was a wealthy captain-mariner and landowner, a fifth genera-tion Waterman in the line from Richard Waterman, who came with Roger Williams to establish the Rhode Island colony early in the seventeenth century. During the French and Indian War Christopher had commanded the privateer sloop *King Hendrick* of Providence. In 1757 he served a term as representative to the General Assembly. Zuriel's mother, Phebe Aborn Waterman (1730–1809), came also from prominent Rhode Island family stock.

Zuriel was the third in age among four children. The eldest was Mary (1752–1846), whose long life with two suc-cessive husbands seems to have been domestic and unmemorable. Next came George (1754–1829). His event-ful life as doctor, public figure, and close companion to his brother is sketched briefly in note 4 of part II. Younger than Zuriel was Phebe (1757–1847). Her long life remains undocumented, except that we know that she never married.[1]

Zuriel's early years before he turned to privateering at age twenty-three are largely a blank. During these years he must have studied medicine, perhaps with his brother, becoming a qualified physician at a young age. He must also have gained his love and talent for high living which are so apparent in the diary. As eldest son, George apparently inherited the bulk of their father's large estate

---

1. Genealogical information is from Donald L. Jacobus and Edgar F. Waterman, *The Waterman Family* . . . , 3 vols. (Hartford: Connecticut Historical Society, 1939–1954), III, 60–64. Other information about Zuriel's life has been gleaned from manuscript materials in the Waterman papers in the Rhode Island Historical Society. Except as specifically noted, all manuscripts referred to below come from this source.

when he came of age. This arrangement seems to reflect the differing temperaments of the two brothers as well as tradition. Zuriel proved to be a great roamer and good-time seeker, as well as an unsuccessful (or unlucky?) money manager.

Judging from Zuriel's letters, prize money (especially to pay off his constant debts) and a chance to "rove the world" were the major incentives which sent him privateering. With apparent anticipation of prize money to come, he wrote to sister Phebe from the *Providence* while moored off Namquit (Gaspee) Point on September 9, 1779, to "tell George that I'd have him sell my gun & Watch & cancel that Note of J. H.'s & other Debts." That cruise did not clear his debts, however, for although the *Retaliation* cruise in 1780 (not described in the diary) netted him £302.2.0 in prize money, he already owed an equal amount and so just broke even. Before that account was closed, he was already another £15.18.0 in debt. In August 1781 major reasons that he did not return home after the *Rambler* cruise were further accumulated debts at home and delays in receiving prize money due him. In a letter to George dated Newburyport, August 12, 1781, he complained of the small amount of prize money he had received in depreciated "Leather Money" from the *Rambler* cruise. He went on to complain that "The Prize, that I wrote you about last March [after the *Hibernia* cruise], that was sold for 1000 soes [sous, French currency not worth much] in Martinique, is yet in dispute, & will be till nex[t] November: If I had got my 1 shares of it I intended to have paid Dr. Wickes; but I have had but barely enough to support me decently since from home. As I know that Dr. Wickes wants the money . . . I desire you wou'd do me the kindness to put to sale the small Lot in Coventry (adjoining Goody Collins's) which you gave me a deed of last Autumn, & also pay my other debts as pr. List," which was attached to the letter. He went on to state that "I am uncertain when I shall be at home again, finding good Company here, & great inclination to rove the World. I am not yet engaged on another

Cruise, but expect to be daily." A month later he sailed on the *Chace* from Salem, having failed to secure a berth on a Newburyport privateer.

Following the *Chace* cruise, the diary ends on January 5, 1782, leaving Zuriel in Boston. He sailed in February, apparently from Salem (since he left a chest there), on another privateer cruise, for on March 14 he wrote to his old friend Zachariah Rhodes from "Lord Howe's Prison Ship" at Charleston, South Carolina, informing Zachariah that he had been captured on February 26 and was being treated well in captivity.[2] His good luck in eluding capture during six cruises from 1779 through 1781 had finally forsaken him. He was probably paroled soon but restricted to Charleston, for on June 6 he officially became a Master Mason in the Solomon Lodge in that city.

By later the same summer, however, Zuriel was living at Edenton, North Carolina, having apparently been released to there by the British (who did not evacuate Charleston until December of that year). Edenton, on Albemarle Sound, though by this time a bustling southern-style town, had been established by New Englanders from Massachusetts Bay Colony. Writing to Phebe on March 7, 1783, Zuriel described the elegance of high society at Edenton and declared that "I do not expect to be at home this some time."

Zuriel was not yet quite done with privateering, either. He wrote to George on May 18, 1783, telling him that early in April "I went out in the Privateer I mentioned to you; we had just got mann'd & waiting for a fair wind to put to sea from Beaufort when we had news of a Peace [signed April 15]. . . . I got back to Edenton April 21st. Since then I have been in this town, where I have a little practice, but intend to go to the westd. about 30 or 40 miles dist. as soon as ever I can." He requested that George "sell all my land, if you have not already done it, & remit me the overplus after paying my debts." He went on to reflect about the past and the future. "I have

---

2. This letter is printed in *The Waterman Family*, III, 64.

been drudging the whole war & all to no purpose, not-withstanding every prudent method I could take; & now I have a fine prospect of a good business if I only had the assistance I ask." So Zuriel planned at last to settle down, to become a gentleman country doctor to the gentleman plantation aristocracy west of Edenton.

But Zuriel's hopes did not materialize. He never raised the money he needed to go to the country, but he did keep up his practice in town and continued to observe closely (though participate in little due to financial distress) the life of the planter aristocracy. In a letter to Phebe dated February 13, 1784, he described, as he put it, "the black side of the Picture." Among other comments, mostly directed toward the idiosyncrasies of southern speech and manners, he observed that "The multitude of Negroes here makes it a scandal for many to work, I mean any work but sewing: For them to see some of my fair countrywomen at hard work, would excite their contempt 20 times where it would their pity once. Tho' I am not of their mind, I cannot see with indifference the sable Sons of Adam made dru[d]ges & worse than dogs of to support their arbitrary Superb *masters, who* are no more belov'd by their Creator than an African is." In this context it is interesting to note that George was soon to play an active role in anti-slave-trade activities in Rhode Island.

This letter of February 13, 1784, reveals the seeds of what was soon to propel Zuriel home to Rhode Island. Besides his growing dislike of southern society, there was the continual burden of "my ill fortune since my absence" and "My inability financially to dress & frolic" so that "the Belles here . . . are all indifferent to me as yet." By December Zuriel was back in Cranston, settling final debts at Edenton by mail.

We know little of Zuriel's life back in Rhode Island except that he did not find his belle there either. Apparently he reestablished his medical practice, as well as his close friendship with George. It is safe to assume also that when he could scrape up the money he had some good times with old friends. An indication of his continuing ability to observe and record events vividly and dramatically comes from an incomplete farcical play manuscript written by Zuriel, perhaps with George's help, probably during this time.[3] The play contains drawing room and barroom scenes and stereotypical characters like the aristocratic Sir William Worldly, the testy old gentleman Sir Snagwood (changed from Crossgrain), Doaty Grumble, Aaron Dump, Jonathan Drawl, Sanctus Satanus, Scrape (a servant), and many others.

On September 20, 1786, a tragedy occurred which cut Zuriel's life short at thirty years. George wrote a manuscript statement (apparently for the *Providence Gazette*) describing the sad event.[4] "Joseph Rhodes Senior desended a Cistern in the distill House to discharge a quantity of Putrid stagnated water; . . . as soon as he arrived to the bottom, he spoke to Fuller who was above, how dreadfully it smells here, I feel faint! he fell immediately, Fuller call'd for help . . . . My Brother and Zachariah Rhodes being at the N. door, ran immediately to assist Mr. Rhodes. Z. Rhodes desended the ladder first, my Brother close after him; . . . they both fell instantaneously on their faces . . . Doctor Rhodes descended the ladder . . . grasped the cape of Z. Rhodes Coat and rais'd him up; . . . in less than half a minute after, Simeon Smith descended the Ladder and brought my brother up." Zachariah Rhodes survived, but Zuriel had suffocated to death, an untimely and ironic twist of landlocked, freak-accident fate for this doctor-privateersman who had so frequently tested the fate of the open sea.

Privateering

Privateering, put simply, was legalized piracy. More precisely, a privateer was a privately owned and operated armed vessel which during wartime received an official commission from a belligerent nation, posted a cash bond

3. The play is in a small collection of Waterman manuscripts in the Harris Collection of the Brown University Library.

4. The *Providence Gazette* story, published on September 23, 1786, is substantially different but was probably based on George's account.

as security against violation of that belligerent's privateering regulations, the rules of war, and the laws of nations, and sailed forth on the high seas to capture enemy shipping (mostly merchantmen), which were brought into harbor as prizes. An admiralty or maritime court conducted a trial to determine the legality of each capture (condemnation proceedings) before ship and cargo were sold at auction and the proceeds divided according to law and the privateer's articles (contract with the crew). The complicated legalities were the theoretical difference between an internationally recognized method of naval warfare with private vessels and the illegal, unregulated, but essentially similar practice of piracy.

Privateering was a familiar and accepted method of warfare to Americans, especially New Englanders, of the Revolutionary era. They had been called upon by Britain to engage in privateering during several colonial wars fought since the late seventeenth century. Now, during the Revolution, they took it up against their mother country even before the Declaration of Independence.[5]

On November 1, 1775, Massachusetts Bay Colony led the way with "An Act for encouraging the Fixing out of Armed Vessells to defend the Sea Coast of America, and for Erecting a Court to Try and Condemn all Vessells

---

5. The following references on privateering upon which the editor has relied are listed in addition to those cited specifically elsewhere in this section: Gardner W. Allen, *Massachusetts Privateers of the Revolution, Massachusetts Historical Society Collections*, LXXVII (1927); Gardner W. Allen, *Naval History of the American Revolution*, 2 vols. (Boston: Houghton Mifflin Co., 1913); Jack Coggins, *Ships and Seamen of the American Revolution* (Harrisburg, Pa.: Stackpole Books, 1969); Thomas S. Collier, *The Revolutionary Privateers of Connecticut . . .*, *New London County Historical Society Records and Papers*, part 4, I, 3–74; Ralph M. Eastman, *Some Famous Privateers of New England* (Boston: privately printed for the State Street Trust Co., 1928); Michael Finefrock (pseudonym for John Nicholas Brown), "Revolutionary Privateering: The First American Navy" (unpublished typescript, Brown University Library, 1961); Edgar S. Maclay, *History of American Privateers* (New York: D. Appleton and Co., 1899); G. F. de Martens, *An Essay on Privateers, Captures, and Particularly on Recaptures . . .*, translated from the French, with notes, by Thomas H. Howe (London, 1801); Ralph D. Paine, *The Ships and Sailors of Old Salem* (Chicago: A. C. McClurg & Co. 1912); Charles O. Paullin, *The Navy of the American Revolution* (Chicago, 1906); Edwin H. Rand, "Maine Privateers in the Revolution," *New England Quarterly*, XI (December 1938), 826-34; Sidney S. Rider, mss. material on the history of privateering in the colony of Rhode Island during the Revolution, Brown University Library, 189?.

that shall be found infesting the same."[6] Citing legal authority for self-defense from both Britain and the Continental Congress, and declaring the immediate need for action since "the Military Tools of these our unnatural Enemies . . . are infesting the Sea Coast with Armed Vessels and daily Endeavouring to distress the Inhabitants, by burning their Towns and destroying their Dwellings with their Substance, plundering live Stock and making Captures of Provision and other Vessells, being the Property of said Inhabitants," the General Court declared that all armed enemy ships and unarmed ships supplying the enemy forces would be subject to forfeiture upon capture by privateers legally commissioned by the colony. Bond was set at £5,000; a system of maritime courts with twelve-man jury trials was established; in the case of recapture of an American vessel previously captured by the British, if the vessel had already been condemned by a British court, the captors received the full value of their prize; if not, the captors received one-third value as salvage rights, while the remainder went to the original owner. On March 18, 1776, Rhode Island, following her neighbor colony's lead, passed essentially the same act but with lower bond (only £2,000) and other minor differences.[7]

Meanwhile, the Continental Congress had been moving more slowly in the same direction. On November 25, 1775, it had resolved that enemy shipping be subject to seizure and, if captured, be legally forfeit, that Congress alone could grant commissions to privateers, and that the colonies should establish maritime courts.[8] Not until March 23, 1776, however, did it get around to passing a definitive act on the subject.[9] Congress now declared that since the British "still continue to prosecute

---

6. The engrossed copy of the act in the State Archives is quoted in full in *Massachusetts Privateers*, pp. 25–31.

7. *Rhode Island Acts and Resolves*, March 1776, pp. 312–20.

8. *Journals of the Continental Congress* (Washington, 1906), November 25, 1775, III, 371–75.

9. *Journals of the Continental Congress*, March 23, 1776, IV, 229–32.

[an unjust war], with their utmost vigour, and in a cruel manner; wasting, spoiling, and destroying the country, burning houses and defenseless towns, and exposing the helpless inhabitants to every misery," the United Colonies were justified in commissioning privateers not only for defensive purposes but also for reprisal and retaliation in kind. Details of commission and bonding were spelled out ($5,000 bond for ships under 100 tons; $10,000 for those over); the colonies were directed to provide courts for condemnation trials. Finally, on April 2 and 3 Congress agreed on a standard commission form and an accompanying set of instructions binding captains to observe the privateering laws, to refrain from unnecessary bloodshed, to sign on "landsmen" for at least one-third of their crews, and to deliver all prisoners to government jails instead of ransoming them.[10]

Massachusetts and Rhode Island quickly revised their laws to conform to the new Continental act and proceeded to turn over most of the responsibility and red tape to the Continental government.[11] Connecticut did not get deeply involved in privateering before the Continental act was passed, so it relied exclusively on Continental commissions except for a small number of coastal vessels.

Two points are worth noting about the justification and purposes of privateering as stated in these laws. First, since the threat was seen to be the British military machine in America and its supply lines, the target for privateering was to be enemy warships and supply ships. There was no call for indiscriminate hunting of any and all British merchant shipping. Second, the purpose was defined in terms of defense and retaliation, not in terms of private profit, though of course that effect of privateering was recognized in the legalities of condemnation proceedings. Each of these observations, when applied to real-life experiences like those of Zuriel Waterman, reveals

---

10. *Journals of the Continental Congress,* April 2 and April 3, 1776, IV, 247–48, 251–54.
11. *Acts and Resolves of the Province of Massachusetts Bay,* April 13 and May 8, 1776; *Rhode Island Acts and Resolves,* May 1776, pp. 41–44. See also Sidney G. Morse, "State or Continental Privateers," *American Historical Review,* (October 1946), LII 68–73.

discrepancies between the stated purposes of government and the actual motivations and decisions of privateers-men on the high seas.

It is worth considering briefly the further history of American privateering. By 1778 Congress was receiving complaints about privateer violations of the rights of trade of neutral countries. In that year Congress warned captains by proclamation that they would receive no American legal protection if they got in trouble, and that they would be liable for damages caused in such incidents.[12] By 1781 Congress' need to protect friendly relations with key neutral nations led it to rewrite its privateer act and instructions to captains incorporating strong warnings about neutral rights.[13]

The United States again used privateers extensively in the War of 1812, but after that time their use quickly diminished worldwide. By 1856 major European naval powers had signed the Declaration of Paris outlawing privateering. The United States (by this time a leading neutral nation) refused to sign, feeling that, as presented, it did not sufficiently guarantee neutral trade rights.[14] Five years later the government in Washington regretted not having signed the declaration when the Confederate States began commissioning commerce destroyers like the *Alabama* to harass Union shipping. When it attempted belatedly to approve the declaration, the United States was rebuffed by Britain and France, both of whom had already recognized the Confederacy's state of bellig-erency.

The declaration issue caused quite a debate in the United States. In 1857 an interesting article appeared sug-gesting that privateering ought to be fostered as a more humane way of fighting wars. The author argued that "war against private property on the high seas is said to be a

12. *Journals of the Continental Congress,* May 9, 1778, XI, 486.
13. *Journals of the Continental Congress,* March 27 and April 7, 1781, XIX, 314–16, 361–64.
14. See Theodore S. Woolsey, "The United States and the Declaration of Paris," *Journal of Social Science,* X (December 1879), 124–35.

rule of the dark ages. . . . So is the monster, war, in all its phases, but least of all when directed against oceanic commerce, since the sacrifice of life is comparatively small, and the loss of property, though often large, is so owned and distributed as to be seldom overwhelming to any one."[15] This is a tempting piece of wishful thinking which might become reality only if privateering could effectively cut off all supplies to armies and navies, thus forcing them to stop killing. Such effectiveness has always eluded privateers, not to mention U-boats.

The article reveals a shift in privateering practice fatal to its own argument, which by the 1850s already had made privateering repugnant enough to be renounced by most naval powers. Beginning with the War of 1812 the old profit motive with all its entangling legalities was gradually abandoned in favor of destruction of prizes at sea.[16] By the time of the Civil War, destruction was the usual practice. Occasionally prisoners were taken, but more often the crew went down with the ship. No claim of humanity can be made for this policy.

When the United States went to war with Spain in 1898, the question of privateering arose again. By now, however, the United States was a great naval power herself and did not need the extra privateer power, so the government unilaterally renounced the use of privateers, in effect accepting belatedly the Declaration of Paris.[17]

That declaration very quickly became a dead letter, however, as the continuing vulnerability of merchant vessels (and passenger liners) in wartime was grimly demonstrated in two world wars by navy submarine commanders who did not concern themselves with the subtle legalities of privateering as opposed to piracy. To them the vague and dubious legality of warfare itself justified their every act, no matter how inhuman.

---

15. "Privateering," *Littell's Living Age*, 2nd ser., XVIII (July–September 1857), 559–60.
16. "Privateers *versus* Volunteer Fleets," *Blackwood's Magazine*, CLXXVI (July–December 1904), 478–89.
17. "No Privateering," *The Nation*, April 28, 1898, pp. 318–19.

The Privateering Experience of Zuriel Waterman

In the course of the diary here published, Zuriel Waterman sailed on five privateer cruises, serving on five different privateers under five different captains. His varying experiences are of interest in and of themselves. As a small segment of a larger American pattern, they are also useful as the basis for generalized speculations about American privateering during the Revolution.

First let us consider Waterman's role on shipboard. On each cruise he signed as ship's surgeon, yet in the diary we are hard put to find evidence that he performed any professional duties. Perhaps he simply did not ordinarily record his professional activities in his personal diary. More likely, since the diary is sufficiently observant of daily detail to make such omissions seem unlikely, he simply did not have much to do as doctor. Thus it appears that, though a regular officer, he fits the category of what Maclay calls " 'gentlemen sailors' . . . tars of exalted degree, and, in many cases, of long pedigree" who went privateering for adventure, fortune, and prestige, but who "were not assigned to the ordinary work of the seaman. . . ."[18]

If Waterman was not busy professionally, what did he do while cruising? While on the *Rambler* he participated twice in prize-seeking forays on the shallop *Katy*. Apart from that, he tells us little about his personal activities. Despite his vivid descriptions of exciting or memorable events (which in the edited diary are somewhat compressed together), the reader has a sense of a good deal of time passing without much really happening. In fact, boredom, though not specifically recognized by Waterman as such, probably was one of his worst enemies during his cruises, as was true with any sailor of the day. Such was the nature of sailing the high seas.

The degree of action and excitement during a cruise depended to a large extent on the character of the

---

18. Maclay, pp. 7–8.

privateer's captain. For Waterman, the contrasting results under different captains may be measured between cruises under Captain Burgess on the *Fortune* and Captain Fuller on the *Rambler*. The former sailed cautiously up and down the far extremities of the Nova Scotia coast, carefully avoiding Halifax, the only area where both the risks of capture and the prospects of taking a valuable prize were great. His crew had to mutiny to persuade him to return to the Halifax area. On the other hand, Fuller hovered close around Halifax, ignoring the danger while awaiting a chance for a big prize. He unfortunately waited too long and lost his ship. Waterman's least productive cruise appears to have been his first. Captain Godfrey of the *Providence* gained nothing by sailing to Newfoundland and then back to Little Egg Harbor. Many of his crew deserted, realizing the futility of the cruise.

No matter what the courage or timidity of the captain, however, it is clear that to a large extent privateering was a game of chance. The pawns in the game included such uncontrollable factors as the weather (especially wind direction, speed, and fog), the time of day (nightfall frequently causing loss of a chase), and the speed, armament, and nationality of the quarry. Although these last factors could determine who captured whom, the latter two frequently could not be positively discovered until the ships were too close to escape one another again. Overall, Waterman's privateers were both lucky and unlucky. Many of the larger ships they chased turned out to be other American privateers. Never in Waterman's experience did one of his privateers capture a really valuable merchantman. On the other hand, neither did any of his ships battle or get captured by a British man of war. The loss of the *Rambler* was less a stroke of bad luck than a running out of overextended good luck so near to Halifax. Thus, Waterman successfully avoided (until after the end of the diary) the cruel prison-ship fate of those who were captured by the British.

The types of prizes Waterman's privateers did capture are interesting to examine in light of stated official justifications and purposes of privateering and of the actual motivations of privateersmen. The diary leaves no doubt that Waterman's chief motive and that of those with him was profit. To argue that cruising off Nova Scotia and in the West Indies was defending the American coastline makes no sense. To argue that Waterman's privateers significantly interrupted, or even attempted to interrupt, the supplying of British forces in America is contrary to fact. Moral bankruptcy might argue, contrary to the expressed motives of the privateersmen, that they were engaging in just retaliation in kind for depredations by the British. A better argument might be made, however, that off Nova Scotia, at least, Waterman's privateers actively subverted both the spirit and the letter of the privateering laws by preying on the coastal trade of poverty-stricken local inhabitants. Though Waterman and other crew members exhibited some sensitivity in individual situations to the immorality of their actions, they did not change their general policy and purpose. From this point of view it is difficult to escape the conclusion that Waterman in fact participated willingly in activities describable only as piracy.

Editing the Diary

The objective in editing this diary for publication has been to shorten a lengthy journal to a readable length by cutting out many less interesting passages (more than a third of the total) while at the same time preserving the tone of the work. That tone might be described as a continuum of mundane everyday events punctuated by some vividly memorable occurrences. Both mundane and memorable events are essentially personal. Still, the Revolution, even in its landmark events, was essentially no more than a huge collage of personal stories such as this.

As noted in the text, there is a sizable nine-month section of diary which presumably is lost rather than unwritten. The manuscript was written in separate booklets (for the different cruises) which later were bound together and have since come partially unbound again. Probably the missing section was bound with the rest but has since come loose and been lost. The question arises as to whether there was additional diary manuscript before and after what we now have. If Waterman did keep a diary previously, it probably did not include privateering. The beginning of the *Providence* cruise has all the hallmarks of a beginning of privateering for him. The first page is begun with a flourish as something decisively new. Also, he kept careful daily records of position, winds, etc., as well as a list of crew members, their ranks, shares, and when they deserted; this scrupulous note-taking practice waned on later cruises. Finally and most telling, he got quite seasick the first few days out, an experience he never repeated. We know that Waterman went on one more privateer cruise (and barely began another) after the diary ends and that he was captured. If he did keep a diary on this cruise, it was lost or confiscated by the British. If he kept a diary in prison, at Edenton, or later back in Rhode Island, there is no trace of it now.

An oddity of the diary is Waterman's occasional use of Latin. There appears to be no particular logic as to when he would switch to Latin or what kinds of thoughts he recorded in that language rather than in English. As a doctor, his professional abilities required a certain amount of understanding and use of Latin. Perhaps on shipboard he wrote occasionally in Latin to keep from getting rusty at it. Rusty or not, his usage is frequently unorthodox and at times impossible to understand. The passages printed (about a third of the total), which were translated by the editor with the expert assistance of the late Noel P. Conlon of the Rhode Island Historical Society staff, were chosen because they did make some sense and seemed to relate to the English text surrounding them.

In the text presented here, spelling and capitalization have been modernized and punctuation has been supplied or changed where needed to make the meaning clear. Dating has been standardized, and except where noted, geographical place names have been modernized.

The editor would like to thank the Rhode Island Sons of the American Revolution, the Rhode Island Daughters of the American Revolution, the Rhode Island Bicentennial Foundation, and the Rhode Island Historical Society for the financial and professional backing which has made this effort possible.

David Swain

Jacksonville, Florida
June 25, 1980

DIARY OF A DOCTOR–PRIVATEERSMAN
1779 TO 1781

I. Cruise on the privateer *Providence*, September 5 to November 19, 1779

[Zuriel Waterman apparently commenced keeping a diary when he first went to sea privateering. In this first recorded cruise, he sailed from Providence, Rhode Island, in the sloop Providence, *commanded by James Godfrey and owned by Robert Stevens of Providence.[1]]*

SUNDAY SEPTEMBER 5, 1779   Went on board the privateer that lay against Fox Point [in Providence harbor] at 4 P.M.; at 6 P.M. came to sail; went down little below Starve Goat Island [in Narragansett Bay], anchored; fair and clear.

MONDAY 6   Fair, pleasant; working upon tourniquets; at 5 P.M. Mr. John Brown[2] and the captain came on board; set sail immediately, the wind S; beat down the river . . . as far as Warwick Neck; came to anchor. Mem. Mustered 52, officers included. . . .

WEDNESDAY 8   This morn the boat went ashore for milk, and Stephen L—— ran away; Captain [of Marines Augustus] Newman and Mr. [Joseph] Allen [prize master] went ashore to find [him], but in vain; he entered as a good seaman and yesterday was ordered aloft; he declined to go; the boatswain drove him up as far as the crosstrees; then he acknowledged he was no

---

1. See Edward Field, ed., *State of Rhode Island and Providence Plantations* . . . , 3 vols. (Boston: Mason Publishing Co., 1902), II, 426.
2. This is almost certainly the prominent John Brown of Providence who made a fortune in the mercantile trade and manufacturing, supplemented during the Revolution by privateering. It is possible that he had a part interest with Robert Stevens in the *Providence*. At any rate, it appears that after the *Providence* returned from this cruise on November 19, 1779, John Brown bought her and dispatched her on December 31 on another privateering venture under the command of Thomas Jackson. See Field, II, 426.

seaman; he had sold ¾ of a share. At night weighed
anchor; went up a mile short of Conimicut Point.

THURSDAY 9   At sunset weighed, the wind WNW, and
went out by Dutch Island. Spoke with 4 boats; they were
Colonel Barton's.[3]

FRIDAY 10   Fair; at 10 A.M. off Gay Head [on Martha's
Vineyard], so called from the various colors of red,
white, yellow, etc.; then saw a schooner standing for us
at 11 A.M.; stood for her, put out all sails, but the wind
died away; at 2 P.M. gave over chase and kept our course
for Holmes' Hole [since renamed Vineyard Haven]; at 5
P.M. spoke with a schooner bound to Boston; informed
us of 30 sail of the Tory refugee [loyalist] fleet lying
at anchor in Holmes' Hole; took in light sails, wind at
WSW, hauled close on the wind; at 6 P.M. saw 2 sail
coming out of Holmes' Hole; at 7 P.M. came to anchor
off Naushon Island; sent the barge ashore; at 11 P.M.
the pilot came off; weighed and got into Woods Hole.

SATURDAY 11   At 10 A.M. got under way from Naushon
and beat through Woods Hole and sent pilot ashore;
at 2 P.M. Quick's Hole [on Naushon Island] bore SSW;
the bow struck a rock once; fair stiff breezes; at ½ past
3 P.M. came to anchor under Clark's Point; at 4 sent
boat to [New] Bedford; at 7 P.M. pilot came on board;
got under way and came to anchor in [New] Bedford
harbor. . . .

WEDNESDAY 15   Course various, intending for the banks
of Newfoundland.

----

3. Colonel William Barton, famous for his capture of British General Prescott near
Newport in July 1777, had in 1778 been severely wounded, so was no longer in active
duty. In 1779 Barton, according to Catherine Williams' biography, "aggravated by
the continual alarms, at Providence, and enormities committed on the shores and
islands of Narragansett bay [by the British], asked and obtained of the Legislature
of the State of Rhode-Island, the command of a few boats for the defence of the coast
of this region. . . ." (Catherine Williams, *Biography of Revolutionary Heroes . . . William
Barton and . . . Stephen Olney* (Providence: published by the author, 1839), p. 87. It was
apparently four of these boats with whom the *Providence* spoke near Dutch Island.

THURSDAY 16   Very heavy gales and large swell from the eastward, wind NE; latitude by observation 39° 18′; very sick. . . .

SATURDAY 18   Gentle gales and pleasant, wind NE; at 5 A.M. saw a ship, gave chase; at 9 A.M. spoke with her, full of soldiers bound to New York; at 12 engaged her; fired about 24 shot at her; left her and stood to the eastward; she had 4 guns; thought, though, she would hurt our cruise, because it would take so many men to man her and look after the prisoners. . . .

[For over two largely uneventful weeks the Providence *sailed northeastward, being held up during part of that time by a storm, until on October 4 it reached the latitude of the southern coast of Newfoundland, whereupon it turned southward again.]*

MONDAY OCTOBER 4   Latitude 47° 14′; at 11 at night, as Mr. [John W.] Smith [captain's clerk] and I lay in a hammock together, head and point, his end of the hammock broke down but did not hurt him much; we lay upon the floor, and little after, Mr. Allen's hammock at the head broke down, and he fell upon my feet; it hurt him considerable.

TUESDAY 5   Very foggy, thick weather; at 6 A.M. saw 11 sail of ships bearing SW by W, bearing 4 miles; they made sail and gave us chase but did not put out their small sails; wind at SSE, we steered NNE; found 1 of the fleet to be a frigate; they left off chasing us at noon and bore east of us; if they had not their convoy, no doubt that they would have taken us. . . .

THURSDAY 7   Saw land the other day just before we shifted our course for the southward, I think last Monday; judged it to be Cape Race [Newfoundland]. . . .

SUNDAY 10   Latitude 40° 30′ [east of Sandy Hook, New Jersy].

MONDAY 11   Fair, warm, and pleasant; early in the morn saw a sloop; set all sail and gave chase and gained upon her slowly; got so nigh at or before night that we gave several bow guns; about sunset she hove to and lay by for us; our captain ordered her boat aboard us; she proved to be the *Isabella*, Captain Levin Tripp, from Baltimore in Maryland bound to Lorient in France, out 22 days, loaded with tobacco; brought no news; out 1st lieutenant went on board; found no contraband goods on board; one of her hands came on board to have his hand dressed which was mashed. . . .

TUESDAY 12   Hodie Dux vapulatus fuit McLoth multi cum rope. . . .[4]

SATURDAY 16   Fair, warm, and pleasant; 1 small shower after dinner, then fair and pleasant; played whackets upon the quarterdeck, and the hands played hot cockles; a fine, warm evening. Latitude 41° 10′.[5]

SUNDAY 17   Caught a dolphin about 11 A.M.; they are the beautifullest fish [*sic*] that ever I saw, long and slender with a forked tail, of a beautiful, variegated green mixed with blue spots; the back fin runs from the neck to the end of the tail. . . .

FRIDAY 22   Fair, fresh gales of wind and a rough sea; saw several flying fish skipping over the water; they made a very pretty appearance; were about as big as a herring; some flew 20 or 30 rods. Latitude 37° 25′ north [near the mouth of Chesapeake Bay]; C[yrus] Williams vapulatus fuit a Duce.[6] A very fine evening.

---

4. Translation: "Today the captain had [either Peter or Solomon] McLoth flogged very hard with a rope."

5. The game Waterman calls whackets most probably is the same as "Whackem," where the players stand in a circle, facing inward, with eyes closed and hands behind their backs. One player runs around the circle with a short length of rope, then quickly puts the rope in a player's hand. That player immediately begins striking the player on his right with the rope and continues to do so while chasing him all the way around the circle. Then the player now possessing the rope begins the game over again. Ionia and Peter Opie, *Children's Games in Street and Playground* (Oxford University Press, 1969), p. 203. Hot cockles is an even less intellectual game of similar nature. It is described as "the sport of giving a person a clout [while his eyes are covered] and having him guess who did it." Opie, p. 293.

6. Translation: "Cyrus Williams was flogged by the captain."

The flying fish now skips o'er the sea
Pursued by dolphin with speed does flee;
But sometimes as he rises in the air,
The birds, they see him and attack him there.
Danger now attacks him on ev'ry side;
The fear of both at once, his cares divide. . . .

SUNDAY 24   Fair, very warm and pleasant; a very fine day and a fine moonshine evening; upon the quarter-deck till 12 P.M.; L[ewis] S. Greene [a volunteer crewman from Pawtuxet] lay down on deck and just got asleep when some of the watch threw a bucket of water upon him; he got up and swore and talked very high. Mem. Hesturnia ille juravit et maledixit plurime, quia J[ohn] W. S[mith] scripsit suum nomen subter primi viridis nomen, sed ille scripsit nomen ejus ita subter articelos *se ipso*. . . .[7]

FRIDAY 29   Calm, warm weather, some cloudy. Mem. Omnes disconti quia non cepimus ullum, et cibus eorum fuit nil tantum 1 libra panis et 1 libra carnis in die, etiam suae rationes spiriti mansae fuerunt cum cepimus tam multos pisces et coryza mansa fuit quatuor dies hi. . . .[8]

SUNDAY 31   A little before sunrise saw a sail bearing S easterly from us; a stark calm; out oars and rowed; . . . at ¼ past 9 A.M. the boat set out and rowed for [the] chase (she being then 1½ leagues from us). . . . Latitude 39° 17'. At noon saw land bearing N to W from us [the New Jersey coast near Great Egg Harbor]; soon lost sight of her, the fog being very thick; at 1 P.M. the boat came back; they got within 1 mile of her when the fog came up very thick, so they lost sight of her; we saw

---

7. Translation: "Mem. Yesterday he swore and reviled copiously, because John W. Smith wrote his name under the first green hand's name, but he wrote his name thus under the articles *himself*," he being a volunteer.

8. Translation: "Mem. Everyone is discontented because we have not taken any [prizes], and our food is nothing but 1 pound of bread and 1 pound of meat per day, and also their rations of spirits were mansae [?] since we have taken so many fish and coryza [?] was mansa [?] these four days."

the land very plain, sandy, low, and woody; saw several whales within shore spouting. At 2 P.M. the fog cleared away; we . . . gave chase to [the vessel] again (Mem. She was a brig), bearing easterly 8 miles distant from us; manned the boat again at ½ past 2. . . . Fired several guns and showed lights at masthead by turns all night as signals for our boat but saw nothing of her. . . .

MONDAY NOVEMBER 1   A very fine morning; saw no land or sail. At 8 saw land bearing NW; at 10 A.M. the boat came back; they got very nigh the brig last night so as to hear the people talk, cut wood, and a dog bark; they judged her to be a British brig; they prepared to board her when a thick fog came on, and they immediately lost sight of her. . . . Saw 2 sail coming out of Egg Harbor, and saw 3 large sail at anchor more to the N and 1 sloop under sail. She gave us chase; we made for her, all hands to quarters. She fired a shot at us; at 3 spoke with her, the *Comet*, Captain Stephen Decatur,[9] of 8 guns, from Philadelphia, cruising. Informed us that the English had evacuated Newport, Rhode Island, last Tuesday after blowing up the courthouse, granary, lighthouses, and their fortification on Tonomy Hill, that Count d'Estaing had cut off the enemy's retreat at Georgia, taken several of their ships and 900 troops at Beaufort, etc. . . .[10]

---

9. This Stephen Decatur, the father of the famous War of 1812 hero, also led a distinguished seafaring career. During the Revolution he successfully commanded five different privateers, of which the *Comet* was the first. After the war he spent many years in the U.S. Navy. See the *Dictionary of American Biography* and Maclay, p. 88.

10. The latter piece of news appears to be unfounded rumor, probably passed along the privateer grapevine before the events had fully transpired. According to Lossing, when Admiral d'Estaing's French fleet and General Benjamin Lincoln's Continental army converged on British-occupied Savannah in September 1779, there were 800 British troops stationed at Beaufort, South Carolina, under a Colonel Maitland. When the French and Americans besieged Savannah on October 4, Maitland's troops were ordered to that city immediately. On October 17 they managed successfully to slip through the siege lines through the swamps in the fog and reinforced the British forces sufficiently so that the very next day, after a furious battle, they were able to break the siege. Lincoln's army soon retreated to Charleston, and d'Estaing's fleet sailed for France. There is no evidence that the British were attempting to retreat anywhere, that there was any French-American action at Beaufort, or that Maitland's troops or boats were captured at or near Savannah. See Benson J. Lossing, *Pictorial Field-Book of the Revolution* . . . , 2 vols. (New York: Harper & Brothers, 1860), II, 528–33; for more detail see John Andrews, *History of the War with America, France, Spain, and Holland* . . . , 4 vols. (London: John Fielding, 1786), III, 307–18.

TUESDAY 2 The 2nd lieutenant of the *Comet* came on board to pilot us into Little Egg Harbor; we beat in by noon; got aground in the harbor on the 1st point of sand; very cold, fair, and clear. Went on shore upon the isle S of the channel with captain, etc., not having set foot on shore before for 50 days. . . .

THURSDAY 4 Went on shore at Foxborough Isle; it has but one wretched house upon it, being mostly a marsh except a small spot of rising ground where the house stands; it is distant 7 miles from a little village called Clamtown [since renamed Tuckerton][11] and fronts the entrance of [Little Egg] Harbor. The house is inhabited by Moses Mullener, his wife, 2 daughters, and a son. John W. Smith got a discharge to go home and went off. About the same time Abel Davis, Joshua Davis, Ebenezer Smith, James Dean, and Samuel Paddleford stole off undiscovered; we went off the isle; A. Davis went off without shoes or stockings on, leaving 2 pair of good stockings and 1 pair of shoes, etc., in his pack. A very cold night. Mem. De Tertio Ordine: Quam illi coquirunt suas panes, et Dux, etc., edit eas. Ha! Ha! Ha![12] To work unloading our vessel to heave down and grave.

FRIDAY 5 Hove down, cleaned and graved one side of the vessel; very cold night; after dark Fredrick Saltman and Joseph Frazio stole off (though a watch was kept) and took a small boat and went off undiscovered.

SATURDAY 6 Hove down, cleaned and graved the other side of the vessel; then to loading again; moderate

---

11. Clamtown was a bustling seaport at this time. With Chesapeake Bay bottled up by the British fleet, privateers and merchantmen alike put into Clamtown to discharge cargoes of all sorts, which were then transported overland to a temporarily landlocked Philadelphia.

12. Translation: "Mem. Of the third order: How they cook their bread, and the captain, etc., devours it. Ha! Ha! Ha!" The meaning of this passage is obscure. Perhaps it refers metaphorically to the crewmen who worked on the ship but then deserted, leaving behind clothing and forfeiting their shares, all to the potential benefit of the captain and officers. Since they had taken no valuable prizes and probably needed the missing crewmen to do so, this interpretation seems less than satisfactory. On the other hand, the statement cannot be taken literally, since ship's bread was not baked fresh on board but was carried in barrels in the form of hardtack.

weather, hazy. Mem. William Norris, John Kelly, and
Joseph Stuart went to Mullener's to get some rum;
Norris came back and went to work; Stuart came back;
Lt. H[arris] asked him why he did not go to work; he
said he was not able (he had several boils); H. said he
was as able to work as to walk about; Stuart said he was
not and was not going to work; H. had a hunting whip
in his hand; he thrashed him around pretty severely
and presently went to look for Kelly with a stick in
hand; he found him squat in the bushes; he gave him
a couple of strokes; K. then sat up and said H. nor his
master would not have used him so once, etc.; H.
repeated his strokes to make him rise, but K. stood it
out for some time; after 20 strokes or thereabouts, H.
left off; K. came to the tent, pulled off his shirt, showed
his back; his shoulders and back were black and blue
and swelled; showing it to H., who gave several more
blows to revive him; he was very groggy. Soon after,
Norris went to the house; Captain Godfrey and Mr.
Newman went there after him and talked and per-
suaded him to come on board, but he answered in an
insolent manner, refusing to come on board; attacked
Capt. Godfrey and Newman; they beat him pretty much
before they got him tied, and then they left him in the
house somewhat groggy; the gunner, etc., went on shore
at night and fetched him off; came to anchor off
Mullener's house. . . .

MONDAY 8   Fair and tolerable pleasant; Capt. Godfrey
went up to Clamtown. . . . Samuel Axtel's brother came
to see him today. . . . They were rowing toward the SE
part of Foxborough Isle when they saw Mr. [John H.]
Friers [ship's master] getting ballast; they then came to
the sloop, bringing a wild turkey he had bought, which
he gave to Mr. Friers and stayed and drank chocolate
and played checkers, delaying the time till after dark;
when he went to go off, his skiff was gone with Sam
Axtel and Ezra Tubbs; he pretended to be surprised
that his brother would use him so and desired to be
put ashore; we put him ashore at Mullener's, where he

had a boat; C[harles] Ward was left at Beach Isle; they could not find him.

TUESDAY 9   Cloudy and rainy; Capt. G. came back last night about midnight from Clamtown; articles very scarce and dear; afternoon clear.

At Egg Harbor:

rum per gal.	80 dollars	potatoes per bu.	12
sugar per lb.	7	shoes 1 pr.	60
coffee per lb.	7	powder lb.	40
snuff per oz.	3	1 silver dollar	30 or 40
rum per gill	3	1 turkey	15

WEDNESDAY 10   Our 1st lieutenant, master's mate, carpenter, gunner, and captain of marines, etc., went ashore at Mullener's; got very high; set the beach afire; captain went ashore to put it out; they came off most of them pretty happy.

THURSDAY 11   Fair and cold. . . . At 9 A.M. weighed going out and came out; wind at west; course in the mouth nighly SE, then turning gradually easterly till got E. . . . At 2 P.M. saw a sail bearing E; gave chase and came up with her very fast; at ½ past 4 gave her a bow gun; she hove to; spoke with her, a prize sloop to the *Comet,* Capt. Decatur, from [St.] Augustine bound to New York with naval stores, taken the 9th inst.; informed that above 20 sail were on the passage from [St.] Augustine to New York, all of them sloops, brigs, and schooners.

FRIDAY 12   Hazy and thick weather, cold; sold our runaway clothes at vendue; amounted to above £100. . . .

SATURDAY 13   Hazy and warmer than yesterday. . . . It was concluded to steer homeward and break up the cruise, the sails and rigging being very weak and old; this was no sooner known by the crew but it diffused a general joy; all melancholy and despondency vanished; it caused more rejoicing than the Saturday night's grog would have done, though it is several weeks since they had any; before this there was so much complaining and discontent that a stranger would have supposed us to be a transport of Tyburn's convicts;[13] even our honest, psalm-singing Taunton men [had] ceased singing their Saturday night hymn for several weeks. . . .

MONDAY 15 At sunrise saw Block Island bearing N by E from us; at 4 P.M. came to anchor in Tarpaulin Cove [on Naushon Island]; cold; the captain, etc., went on shore to Robinson's and pretended to be a British sloop and under pretense were treated very kindly with cider, beefsteaks, etc.; [Robinson] told them that Newport was evacuated by the British troops 20 days ago (the same time that Capt. Decatur told us it was); professed himself to be a very great friend to [the British] government; before they told him they were British, he said he had nothing to spare, but afterwards he offered to bring 2 sheep, sauce, etc. . . .

THURSDAY 18 Very cold morn, fair and clear; at 11 A.M. weighed and went to beating again up Sakonnet passage; wind northerly; got as far as Warwick Neck; got some milk; at 10 A.M. weighed and beat again; got aground S side of Conimicut Point; very cold.

FRIDAY 19 At 2 o'clock beat again; . . . at 4 A.M. got up to the wharf; most of the hands immediately quit the vessel except the officers, who stayed to get out the guns and unbend the sails. Thus ended our tedious cruise after having been on board 75 days; all got home well in body but bitterly cropsick; I got home about 6 o'clock; all friends very well and affairs in good order, for which thanks be to God. . . .

II. At home near Pawtuxet, November 20, 1779, to April 22, 1780

[Following the cruise on the Providence, *Waterman spent several months at home before embarking on another privateering venture. During this period he continued faithfully making entries*

13. Tyburn was then the place of public execution in London, now within Hyde Park.

*in his diary. Besides cataloging his travels of professional duty
as a physician between home, Pawtuxet (part of Cranston), and
Providence, Waterman describes vividly certain episodes of his
rather wild bachelor-aristocrat social life. Nothing eventful occurred, however, until he had been home for over two weeks.]*

THURSDAY DECEMBER 9, 1779 Fair and pleasant; went
to Providence; it being Thanksgiving Day, came back
to Pawtuxet. John Aborn came home; he went out to
sea last December 22, sailed for North Carolina, from
there to Surinam; he got in the river where lay a British
cruiser who chased him out of the river; he escaped
her and bore away for Martinique; got within sight of
the island when a tender took him (he having sprung
his mast, carrying away his boom, etc.); he was carried
aboard the *Elizabeth,* of 74 guns; for 5 months was
treated very well, lived with the gunner, etc.; was in the
fight that Byron had with d'Estaing; 6 British ships were
very much shattered;[1] they were very sickly aboard;
Israel Arnold died aboard. In September he got to
Martinique in a French cartel; from there he got to
Nantucket, etc. . . .

[Nothing eventful occurred for about three weeks.]

MONDAY 27 Very fair, warm, and pleasant; went to
Providence; at night went to Brown's with Z[achariah]
Rhodes, J. Aborn, S[tephen] Fenner, J. Harris, and
J. Batty. We intended to have a dance there but were
disappointed, so we kept it up all night playing
cards, etc.

TUESDAY 28 Cloudy and snowy all day; keeping it up
at Brown's; about noon J. Harris and J. Batty went away;

---

1. It was common for American prisoners who were not sent to prison ships to
be forced (or bribed) into service in the British Navy. During this engagement, which
took place on July 6, 1779, Admiral d'Estaing successfully defended French possession of the West Indian island of Granada, which he had captured just two days before,
badly mauling Admiral John Byron's British fleet, but himself losing a large number
of killed and wounded. Shortly afterwards, when d'Estaing sailed for Savannah (see
note 10 of part I above), the British retook the now undefended island. See Coggins,
pp. 144–45; Andrews, III, 302–7.

the rest of us stayed to dinner; got away from Brown's about sunset; the reckoning was distributed by the goddess Chance in the following manner, viz.: Z.R. 155, J.B. 100, S.F. 88, Ego 70, J.H. 55, J.A. 23. . . .

FRIDAY 31   Received a letter from Dr. Clark intimating that I might join the *Argo*.

SATURDAY JANUARY 1, 1780   Went to Providence; saw Capt. [Silas] T[albot]; agreed to go in the *Argo*. . . .

[Nothing eventful occurred for over three weeks.]

TUESDAY 25   Fair and very cold; went to the G. Hospital to get medicines for the sloop *Argo,* delivered to me by young Dr. Bowen; dined with him at the hospital.[2] Mem. A very fine young gentleman. Tea and spent the evening at W. Potter's; lodged at Franklin's; Mr. Franklin and lady sleighing; played cards with Miss S., a very agreeable young lady.

WEDNESDAY 26   Fair but very cold; breakfast aboard the *Argo;* was informed that Col. Talbot received a letter from Congress to discharge the *Argo* in consequence of the owner of the *Argo* is applying to Congress for her.[3] Officers concluded to have a bange tonight; met

2. There were several doctors at this time among the members of the prominent Bowen family. This "hospital" functioned during the war, mainly to inoculate against and to treat smallpox, in University Hall, an imposing structure built in 1770 by John Brown as the new home of the College of Rhode Island (later renamed Brown University).

3. The *Argo*, a small sloop armed with twelve six-pounders, had been captured from its New York loyalist owners early in 1779 and came into the ownership of John Brown. She was loaned to the Continental Congress during 1779 for use as a naval vessel under the command of Colonel Silas Talbot against British cruisers which were harassing American shipping along Narragansett Bay and Long Island Sound. After several successful cruises, she was apparently preparing for yet another in January 1780 when John Brown requested that she be returned to him for his private use. Talbot, who had not received promotion to a larger ship as he felt he deserved, decided to resign from the Navy and stay with the *Argo*. On April 14, 1780, the *Argo* sailed on a privateer voyage with Talbot as captain, without Zuriel Waterman. See William J. Morgan, *Captains to the Northward . . .* (Barre, Mass.: Barre Gazette, 1959), pp. 179–81; Field, II, 427. Silas Talbot's outstanding naval career, already a full one, was at this time just beginning. See *Life and Surprising Adventures of Captain Talbot . . .* (London: Barnard and Sultzer, [1803]); Henry T. Tuckerman, *Life of Silas Talbot . . .* (New York: J. C. Riker, 1850); *Historical Sketch . . . of the Life of Silas Talbot . . .*, edited by H. Caritat (New York: G. and R. Waite, 1803).

Lt. Springer; went with him to Bradford's Tavern; found nigh a dozen officers there; drank several bowls of grog and lots of cider there; at night went on board the *Argo;* began our frolic with several stout bowls of grog and toddy, raw drams, slings, etc., singing, roaring, etc., till we got too big for the cabin to hold us and then sallied out in the street, but did not forget to carry a bottle of rum with us, it being exceeding cold and about 8 o'clock; all in good spirits and good spirits in us—not a man of us would flag thus accoutered; we went along street shouting and singing and now and then, to cheer our hearts, stop and take a drink; the word was *Argo!* By this word we raised several of our companions, and so recruited, our company went over the bridge, got a Negro fiddler, and proceeding up town went into a house to have a dance, but a woman was sick there, so we went along further over the mill bridge and went in a house to make our frolic there, but they had got the start of us and had a frolic of their own; one of the women was tumbling to pieces; this business being above our capacity in our present condition, we thought fit to pack off; so went off like so many kegs of rum, tumbling down every now and then, but that did not disconcert us so but that we rose again; stopped at the house where S____y S____r was kept by W____m R____ll but made no tarry there and away; at length we all meet at ____Jencks' Tavern and made out this list, viz.: R. Mumford, E. Talbot, W. Bucklin, myself, John Gifford, L. Mumford, J. Pollinshow, _____ Lawrence, L. Olney, _____ Burkett, _____ Owens, _____ Cozzens; went to fiddling and dancing, but R.M. [and] L.O. got so that they were carried to bed, and W.B. was no better; he sat asleep and nodding by the fire for 3 or 4 hours and then got so as to steal off and go home; the others kept it up and intended to have a supper, but the landlord affronting us, we called for the bill, disputed it, and several of us came off; his bill was this, viz.:

4 double bowls of grog	72 dollars
8 mugs of cider	16 ”
a rasher	4 ”
2 slings	7 ”
a chair broke and fire and candles	21 ”
	120 ”

We kept our own account and had but 4 mugs of cider and 3 bowls of grog, no slings, but one rung of a chair broke, and his rasher but a small bit of mutton no bigger than one's finger. I went on board with J. Pollinshow; could not get my boots off; slept a very little, it being 4 o'clock.

THURSDAY 27   Very cold but fair day; about 5 o'clock this morning E. Talbot, L. Mumford, and L. Olney came on board pretty high; they brought fire from the house with them and made several fires in the street as they came along; after they got a drink again, they sallied out for more fun, carrying a coffee pot of strong sling with them; a little after 7 they came on board again, having took a sentry's gun away from him and performed several more exploits; I dressed a man's foot that was scalded last night aboard the *Argo*. . . .

SATURDAY 29   Severe cold, said to be the coldest day that has been this winter; at night with company at A. Aborn's till 10 drinking mulled cider; lodged with John Aborn.

SUNDAY 30   Fair and warm, a very pleasant day; did not rise till 11 o'clock; went home with my brother [George].[4]

4. George Waterman (1754–1829) was, like his brother, a physician. As the elder of the two, he seems to have inherited the substantial landholdings in Cranston and Scituate of his father Christopher Waterman. George was prominent in local public affairs. In 1778 he was on a committee to raise troops in Cranston. After the war he served as tax assessor, as deputy and then representative from Cranston, and as town moderator for several years. In 1789–1790 he served in the state militia, first as a major, then successively as adjutant general and commissary general. See Jacobus and Waterman, III, 60–64. It is apparent from the extant family papers and Zuriel's diary that the relationship between the two brothers was quite close.

MONDAY 31   Fair, exceeding cold last night; a little
snow; went to Providence; never underwent so much by
cold before; froze my left ear, it being to windward;
came home at night; this month has been exceeding
cold; all the bay froze over; can go on the ice to
Newport.

[Nothing eventful occurred for almost two weeks.]

SATURDAY FEBRUARY 12   Fair, warm; went to Mr.
Knight's[5] to the court appointed there for the trial of
_____ Williams at the complaint of V. Joy, he having
caused an uncommon swelling about her waist; likewise,
2 girls more got married to one Mr. S. Fenner [one of
Waterman's drinking friends]; the t[own] sergeant went
for him, brought him by force to Kingston; there he
refused to do anything about the matter; was sent to
Providence jail. This affair being over, several of us
called for a room, drinked and kicked around, broke
down the landlord's bed; had supper; some drunk, vom-
iting; about 6 of us turned in; left Col. Potter there,
who kept it up all night. . . .

[For over a week nothing eventful occurred.]

TUESDAY 22   Cloudy at night, rain; came home; today
Uncle Thornton received a letter from [cousin] Chris-
topher [Waterman][6] dated Edenton, North Carolina,
January 5, 1780, intimating that he was taken off His-

---

5. This may be Nehemiah Knight, a prominent Cranston resident who was friendly
with the Watermans. After the war Nehemiah was for several years (1803–1808) U.S.
senator from Rhode Island. His son, Nehemiah Rice Knight, a political (anti-Federalist)
friend of George Waterman, who also married a Waterman, held several important
public offices, including those of governor of Rhode Island (1817–1821) and U.S.
senator (1821–1841). See *The Waterman Family*, III, 62; *Biographical Cyclopedia of Representative Men of Rhode Island* (Providence: National Biographical Publishing Co., 1881),
pp. 212–13.
6. In a confusing arrangement of names, Zuriel's cousin Christopher was the son
of his uncle Zuriel, who was the brother of his father Christopher. See *The Waterman
Family*, III, 144. There is no evidence in Zuriel's letters that Christopher was still in
Edenton when Zuriel lived there between 1782 and 1784 (see Introduction).

paniola by a privateer from Jamaica, the master, Lowry Aborn, carried in port, and himself and Edward Sheldon put on board a Bermudian vessel bound to N. Carolina, that Edward was listed for 3 months to go to Georgia and himself shipped on board of a vessel bound to the West Indies. . . .

[For another three weeks nothing eventful occurred.]

WEDNESDAY MARCH 15   Fair, warm, and pleasant; went to Providence; was offered Dr. berth on board the *Lively;* did not agree to go; offered but as much as a prize master; came home with J. Randall; lodged at Mrs. Harris', who was exceeding sick.

THURSDAY 16   Waked this morn at 5 o'clock, but before I could get downstairs, Mrs. Harris died. . . . Saw Lowry Aborn, just got home; was taken last December and carried into Jamaica; got away from there in a Dutch vessel.

FRIDAY 17   Cloudy and cold. . . . Watched with A. Thornton, N. and H. Brown with the corpse of Mrs. Harris.

SATURDAY 18   Fair; Mrs. Harris buried. . . .

[For another two weeks nothing eventful occurred.]

SATURDAY APRIL 1   High wind and warm; today was appointed to be a great fox hunt after a black fox in the neighborhood; 30 or 40 gentlemen with hounds were coming out of Providence; the fox hunters met to hunt the fox, but the gentlemen did not come from Providence, so the fox hunters found themselves to be April Fools. Spent the evening at Mr. Brown's with George Aborn, Stephen Remington, R[euben] Daley, etc.; broke up at 12. Last night 3 men robbed Nathaniel Spague.

SUNDAY 2   Fair, cool, and windy. . . . Adjutant T. Waterman was apprehended today and A. Andrews yesterday upon suspicion of robbing N. Sprague. . . .

TUESDAY 4   Fair, warm, and very pleasant. . . . Yesterday T. Waterman turned state's evidence and accused Nathan Carpenter as accomplice, and last night he was taken at Bristol out of bed from his wife he had lately married and carried to Providence. Today he was carried home to get the money which he had hid in a sandbank. He was brought along handcuffed upon a horse through his native place, a most shocking sight.

WEDNESDAY 5   Fair, warm, and pleasant; to Providence; saw the prisoners; Stephen Fenner there but has the liberty of the yard. . . . Morgan O'Brien, an Irishman, was flogged 30 lashes for stealing 3½ yards of broadcloth. Mr. Beverly, the jailor, gave him a gill of rum before he was flogged; he begged earnestly for ½ of a gill more: "Dear Mr. Beverly, only let me have one-half gill and I will pay you the money as soon as ever I get it, indeed I will, Mr. Beverly. Mr. Beverly, you are the best friend I have in the world," etc. When he was brought to the whipping post and stripped and Mr. Beverly was tying him up: "Dear Mr. Beverly, don't tie my hands so hard. Oh! Mr. Beverly! Mr. Beverly! you hurt me. Oh Mr. Beverly! Mr. Beverly! Mr. Beverly! don't tie my hands so high, my dear Mr. Beverly. Mr. Beverly, my jewel, don't tie my hands so high," etc. After tying his hands, Mr. Beverly proceeded to read the judgment of court, reading the paragraph "that Morgan O'Brien was convicted of stealing." Says Paddy, "Ah, poor Morgan! and have you come to this?" Then reading further, "that he must pay such a fine or be sold for a term not exceeding a year." Says Paddy, "Ah, poor Morgan! then you must be sold like a Negro, for I'll be d____ned if I can get the money; here, take my coat and sell it off my back first; I'm a poor fellow and have no friends." Then Mr. Beverly took the cat to whip him. "Ah, Mr. Beverly, is it you that is going to whip me? I did not know that." Then, while he was flogged, he would hang back his head and let his hair fall on his back. "My dear Mr. Beverly, strike higher, do, my Mr. B., my jewel," etc. As soon as done there, says he, " 'Tis done, now shoot me, shoot me, kill me. I don't want to live," etc. "Mr. Beverly, you are my best friend I have in the world." When asked where his parents lived, says he, "Some live in Pennsylvania and some in Carolina, and I have a very good uncle living in the Jerseys. . . ."

SUNDAY 9 Warm, rain in the morn. Mem. Last Wednesday halted at T____l W[aterma]n's with Z. R[hodes] as coming from Providence. Dialogue. Scene: the parlor, Miss L.P. (cousin, companion, contemporary, and housemaid to Miss C.) sitting, reeling yarn. Enter Dr. W. and Z.R. "Servant, Miss L." "Your servant, gentlemen. Sit down." Enter Miss C. "Your most obedient, madam." Miss C.: "Your servant, gentlement. L., I think you've got a very dirty hearth." Miss L.: "I was waiting for the boy to put on a log." After a little talk, enter C.'s father and brother. Then the talk mostly upon the late theft. After the affair was canvassed over, Miss C., elucidating N[athan] C[arpenter]'s character, said, "Well, I have heard such a thing before about N.C. A gentleman told me that he (N.C.) destroyed a letter and kept the money that was sent by him, pretending that the letter was lost. Mistress T____r (that lives with his brother N.) said that he came there last Sunday and acted very odd indeed. She said that he jumped off and on his horse 3 times. He rode by here the same day; he looked very pale and so dejected that I wondered what should concern him so. He has always been a bad fellow and now he has come to this—*And what won't Pride and LUST bring anybody to.*" Mem. N.C. kept company with her (Miss C.) once and told his friend of it. His friend got affronted with him and told the secret (no ways laudable to Miss C.'s character). N.C. was threatened with prosecution, but he persisting in the assertion, they dropped the affair. . . .

TUESDAY 11   Set out for Providence about 10, intending to go on board the *Argo;* mistook another vessel for her;[7] coming off the wharf, met S. J____n, who told me that Uncle S. A____n had got a berth for me at New London as chief surgeon. . . .

THURSDAY 13   Fair, warm, and pleasant; at 9 set out for New London with Lowry Aborn; dined at Jonathan Dean's; at night got as far as Hyam's (28 miles); went in, asked a girl who was spinning if they kept a public house. "We used to," says she in a squeaking tone. Then she turns to a little boy, scolding "Go 'long and fetch some brush." "Do you speak to me, ma'am?" says he, imitating her voice. Then we asked again, "Do you entertain travelers here, ma'am?" "We do sometimes" (squealing). Here Mr. Hyam come in and informed us it was a public house; ate a hearty supper of fried bacon, coffee, cider; ate up a johnny cake 1½ [feet] long; very good lodgings. . . .

SUNDAY 16   [In Groton.] Cold, cloudy; went to meeting; no priest there; the deacon and some members of the meeting got up, exhorted, prayed, sung psalms, cried—sighed—groaned. Just after a prayer, John Allen (a person insane) got up and says, "I want to buy a bushel of wheat; if any person know of any to be sold, I'd be glad if they'd speak." But this was not answered, and so they proceeded to singing; after singing, he endeavored to mend the matter but made it worse. Very rainy and cold. . . .

TUESDAY 18   Fair; went to New London; engaged to go in the *Retaliation;* saw John Rice. In the evening drinked punch with John Rice, L.A., and Mr. Chubb, a Continental lieutenant; drank 4 bowls; all of us pretty well by the head; introduced to Dr. Wickes; invited by him to a dance; went with L.A. to Mrs. Rice's; joked

---

7. According to Edward Field (see note 3 above), the *Argo* sailed as a privateer on April 14. Why Waterman was unable to find the *Argo* on April 11 is not clear. Perhaps she did as the privateer *Providence* did in 1779, spending several days on a kind of shakedown cruise within Narragansett Bay before putting out to sea.

with L.A; overheard by a lousy scoundrel who informed
the company of it; after the company broke up, Mrs.
Rice informed, he afterwards told L.A. several things
about the company to undervalue it: that they were a
parcel of old maids, a lower class, etc.; lodged at Mrs.
Rice's. . . .

*[By April 22 Waterman was back in Pawtuxet. There is a large
missing section in the diary from April 23, 1780, through
February 2, 1781. From other evidence, we know that Waterman did make an apparently successful cruise on the privateer
sloop* Retaliation *(twelve guns, sixty men), Captain Elisha
Hart, returning to New London by the beginning of September
1780 at the latest.[8] Following that, he presumably returned
home and then went to Newburyport, Massachusetts, from whence
he sailed on another privateer cruise, which by February 1781
had taken him to the West Indies.]*

III. Cruise on the privateer *Hibernia*, February 3 to March 22, 1781

*[After the missing section of the diary, we rejoin Waterman in
the midst of a privateer cruise in the West Indies on the schooner*
Hibernia *(ten guns, fifty men) from Newburyport, Massachusetts,
commanded by Captain John O'Brien.[1] On February 3 they
appear from the navigational evidence in the diary to be at a
port on the east side of Guadeloupe.]*

SATURDAY FEBRUARY 3, 1781   Small showers of rain this
morning. In the forenoon landed our prisoners, 15 in
number, besides Mr. Jefferson [a crewman], who went
to the hospital. . . . Went ashore in the afternoon; took
a view of the town; had been burnt down 7 months ago;

8. See Collier, part 4, I, 17, 30. The evidence that Waterman made this cruise is
a statement of accounts current of Zuriel Waterman with Joseph Hart of Saybrook,
Connecticut, in the Waterman papers, Rhode Island Historical Society. Entries were
made on July 14, 1780, concerning shares in prizes captured by the *Retaliation*, Captain Elisha Hart, and the apparently settled account was signed by Joseph Hart on
August 29.

1. John O'Brien purchased the schooner *Hibernia* in 1779 at Newburyport. On June
9 of that year he sailed on a privateer cruise which proved quite successful. Waterman's cruise was probably O'Brien's second on the *Hibernia*. See Maclay, p. 62.

they were rebuilding it and digging away the hills that are all around and in the middle of the town.[2] I went to the hospital and saw Mr. Jefferson; the sick were exceeding well treated; the hospital is a fine, large building situated on a hill; it is long and has 2 wings. 2 French doctors came on board, 1 a mulatto, the other white; the latter got drunk in going ashore; he was angry with 2 Negros that were rowing him ashore and flogged them all the way with his fist; he got in a very high passion and fell in the water and like to have drowned but got in again; as soon as they got ashore, the Negroes left him, and he fell into the water again but was taken out almost drowned. At night, it being calm, at 7 we weighed and rowed out of the harbor; then a small breeze took us; we steered for St. Pierre in Martinique.

SUNDAY 4   Squally and rainy when against Dominica, which appeared very mountainous; at 9 A.M. made Scotts Head on our starboard bow; at noon got nigh the west side of Martinique; the mountains very ragged and broken with fine rills of water running into the sea, all the steep hills except precipices being cultivated, with Negro huts on the tops and sides and in the valleys little villages of Negro huts; on the tops of the hills some windmills to grind cane; some cannon were planted along shore; at sunset we moored before St. Pierre within a stone's throw of the shore. The *Holker*, brigantine, a privateer from Philadelphia, came in just before us and brought in 2 prizes, one a brigantine from Ireland, the other the *Longsplice*, a noted privateer schooner of 10 guns from Antigua. It was told us that Admiral [Sir George] Rodney made a descent [on December 15, 1780] upon St. Vincent with 3,000 men but met with a great repulse, the French driving his

2. Though there is no evidence that the British burned any French cities in the West Indies during this seven-month period, the whole island chain had suffered tremendous destruction at the hands of hurricanes in October 1780. See Andrews, IV, 107.

men in the boats with bayonets, that the British in the islands were greatly chagrined at it, blaming Rodney very much. . . .[3]

TUESDAY 6   Weather warm and variable. At noon Captain Robert Cheine [of a prize captured by the *Hibernia*] went on board an English flag of truce bound for St. Lucia, giving his parole to Captain [John] O'Brien [of the *Hibernia*], to be null when Captain Jeremiah O'Brien [John's brother] should be exchanged for him or, if not possible to release him, to exchange some other equal rank with himself. In the afternoon went ashore and went up the high hill back of the town; saw the fields of coffee, orange groves, tamarind trees, etc.; very steep up the hill; went up by steps all the way; got certain intelligence that the *Hannibal,* privateer, was overset in a squall bound from New York to the West Indies; she was taken last autumn when on a cruise from Newburyport, commanded by Captain Jeremiah O'Brien.[4] Very hot.

WEDNESDAY 7   Weather as yesterday. . . . At 11 A.M. see a brigantine beating in; believe it to be the *Crowlane,* our last-taken prize; at 12 at noon our boat and Mr. Maly went on board; about midnight the brigantine moored before the town northward of us; she had seen no sail since we took her.

THURSDAY 8   Weather as before, viz., hot and mostly fair with small showers, the mountains just back of the town being constantly covered with clouds.

FRIDAY 9   Weather as yesterday; this evening G. Pool

---

3. This was actually a single, relatively insignificant British defeat among a series of successful forays during this period against fleets and islands belonging to France, Spain, and Holland. See Andrews, IV, 33–38, 66–73, 129–36; Coggins, pp. 191–96.

4. Brothers John and Jeremiah O'Brien had built the *Hannibal* (20 guns, 130 men) together at Newburyport in 1780 for use as a privateer. They shared command on her first voyage. Later that year, in September, while under Jeremiah's command, she was captured after a 48-hour chase by two frigates. Captain and crew were all put aboard the British prison ship *Jersey* at New York. After about six months (which is after the date of this diary entry) the crew was exchanged, but Jeremiah was transferred to Mill Prison, Plymouth, England. Quite soon he successfully escaped to France and home. Maclay, p. 61.

beat Tom Haines very bad. 'Tis reported with confi-
dence that the British have taken St. Eustatius from
the Dutch. . . .[5]

MONDAY 12   Weather as yesterday, somewhat better;
this afternoon the *Holker* came in and brought with
her a cutter of sixteen guns which she took after three
hours engagement; the cutter lost her captain and 5 men
killed and 7 wounded, the *Holker,* 1 killed and 2 or
three wounded; the cutter was from Liverpool; at sunset
they landed the prisoners; they were attended by a
numerous mob who shouted and hooted at them. . . .

THURSDAY 15   Ballasting and loading our vessel for a
cruise. The *Dean,* privateer, Captain [Elisha] Hinman,
and the *Protector,* Captain [John Foster] Williams, came
in here today;[6] heard that the [privateer] *Randolph*
engaged 2 English privateers and got badly mauled and
lost many men, just escaping them, and had got into
Fort Royal [since renamed Fort de France, Martinique]
harbor. Today our prize sailed for Fort Royal, being
sold there for the use of the [French] Royal Navy; sent
our Negroes ashore to sell.

FRIDAY 16   Stowing and tetivating [?] our vessel. At night
our people came from the brig *Crowlane* at Fort Royal,
all except Mr. McCann and 2 more; heard that Britain
had declared war against all the confederated neutral
armed powers [the League of the Armed Neutrality].[7]

---

5. This was accomplished on February 3 without significant opposition soon after
word of the declaration of hostilities between Britain and Holland reached the West
Indies, and before the Dutch had time to prepare any defense of this center of illicit
(while Holland had been neutral) war goods trade with America. According to Coggins (p. 196), "The booty was tremendous. Merchandise, crammed in a long row of
storehouses, was valued at more than £3,000,000. Over 150 merchant ships were taken,
and a convoy of 30 more which had left the island two days before was chased and
captured also."

6. The *Dean* (twenty guns) was Hinman's first privateer command after a truncated
career in the Navy, during which he commanded the *Cabot* and the *Alfred.* After the
Alfred was captured in 1778 by the British, sending him temporarily to Forton Prison,
Portsmouth, England, he never received another ship to command. So eventually he
quit the Navy for privateering. Collier, part 4, I, 66–67; Morgan, *passim.*

7. The league was never really neutral, and after the British declared war on league
member Holland (December 20, 1780) for, among other things, illegal war goods trade
with America through St. Eustatius, it was not long before the rest of the league was
dragged into the conflict.

SATURDAY 17   Morning cool as a morning in New England in October and no rain; every other morning that we have been here before it has rained; a large fleet passed by here; supposed it to be the English fleet from St. Eustatius.

SUNDAY 18   Weather as usual; in the morning went aboard Captain _____ ['s ship] and bled him; in the afternoon went ashore to the American coffee house; saw Dr. Rawson; he came here in the *Protector*, surgeon's mate; drank coffee with him, etc.

MONDAY 19   Weather as usual; this morning our men grumbled and refused to work because they could not get their prize money before they went out; Captain O'Brien sent them aboard the *Protector*, a state ship. The boatswain was one; there were 6 or 8 in all; we are not likely to receive our prize money till we have heard orders from Congress. . . .

THURSDAY 22   Early in the morning went to church with Dr. Rawson; it was very elegant: The floor blue and white marble in checkers; the room painted all around with scripture history such as St. Michael overcoming the old dragon, the miracle of the five loaves and 2 fishes; there was a very beautiful altar with a large golden cross on the table on the altar supported with angels with beautiful carved work around it; opposite the altar was the Virgin Mary holding the child Jesus in her arms; they were made of alabaster and had each a crown of gold; the crowns were not solid but composed of bars; their crowns were set with precious stones; the Virgin Mary was about 2½ [feet] long and the child Jesus about 15 inches. The church was divided in 2 parts; there was an openng about 10 feet square between them with a network of iron that covered the whole; a green curtain hung on the other side, before the grating; I looked through a little space the curtain did not quite cover; I saw 2 or 3 women nuns kneeling at prayer; it appeared to be beautifully ornamented. While we were in the church, a young lady came in and kneeled down before the altar; 2 more came in, and 2 children went to the marble basin of holy water, dipped their fingers in, and crossed themselves on the forehead and breast; we also crossed ourselves with holy water. From there we went to another church where they were at divine service but had almost done. They were singing when we went in; as soon as they stopped, they all fell on their knees to prayer, the priest pronouncing aloud; that being soon over, they fell to singing again; that ended, a small bell rung for about 1½ minutes, during which time they were all on their knees at prayer; that over, they came out of church. We breakfasted at our lodgings; Dr. Rawson went aboard the *Hibernia* and dined; in the afternoon I went with him aboard the *Dean;* saw Lt. R. Arnold; then aboard the *Protector;* was introduced to Dr. Clark, a young gentleman from Connecticut; Mr. [R] Mumford [one of Waterman's drinking friends from Providence] and several others came aboard from the *Dean;* we spent the evening very merry till 11 and then went to bed.

FRIDAY 23   Stayed aboard the *Protector* till 11 and then went aboard the *Hibernia* with Dr. Clark and Mr. [Edward] Preble. . . .[8]

MONDAY 26   This morning the *Holker* came in with a fine ship prize loaded with dry goods and provisions; her sterling invoice was £12,000.

TUESDAY 27   Weather as common; Sunday last being Shrove Sunday, that and yesterday and today are three great holy days with the inhabitants; every night they have a dance on the beach with music, etc. Captain Simmons in a drogher here had got several of our people aboard his vessel that had signed our articles; Captain O'Brien demanded them of him; Simmons said if they were aboard, Capt. O'Brien should have them. Capt. Simmons went aboard in Capt. O'Brien's boat

---

8. Edward Preble, then only nineteen years old, was a midshipman on the *Protector.* He went on to a distinguished naval career, especially during the war with Tripoli. See the *Dictionary of American Biography* and Maclay, p. 133.

with Capt. O'Brien and six men; as soon as they got
aboard, Simmons struck Capt. O'B. and called for his
arms and asked if there were no handspikes aboard;
several others struck Capt. O'B. and stunned him and
hove him overboard; several others struck Mr. Howell
very badly on the head and shoulder at the same time
and struck and threw all overboard except the steward,
he not being able to swim; they pelted him on the deck.
Mr. Howell was heaved in the boat, stunned; a French-
man jumped in the boat after him, beating him till H.
got an oar and drove him out of the boat and then cut
the painter; 2 more got in the boat with him. The captain was hove over the other side, stunned; as soon as
he knew where he was, he swam toward their vessel and
got aboard, they endeavoring to hinder him; at last
they set him and the steward ashore. 4 were beat and
bruised badly; in the fray Simmons ordered his men
to kill them and heave them overboard; the captain lost
his hat and some money.

ASH WEDNESDAY 28   First day of Lent; weather as usual;
Capt. O'Brien settled the affair with Simmons, the latter acknowledging his fault and begging pardon and
paid damages; in the afternoon put to sea; to and fro,
Dominica to M [artinique].

THURSDAY MARCH 1   Fair and hot; sailed along the
west side of Dominica; was hailed by the fort at Scotts
Head; saw 4 sail of small vessels that kept within us,
close ashore.

FRIDAY 2   Fair and hot; saw Antigua, Nevis, St. Kitts
[St. Christopher], St. Eustatius, and sailed by the west
side of Saba [on a northwesterly course]. . . .

WEDNESDAY 7   Fair, warm, and pleasant; a smooth sea,
light airs of wind; today being a good time for duck-
ing (it blowing hard when on the Tropic [of Cancer]),
all were ducked that crossed it going to the W.I. I was
the first called up (*a instigatione* Mr. Maly); it is performed thus: Two handspikes lashed horizontal and

parallel; I sat on the lower, the upper one being against my breast (I refusing to pay anything more); was lashed to them, hoisted up to the weather foreyardarm, and giving three cheers, they let me go by the run in the sea, doing thus 3 times. Course due north; latitude 27° 03'.

THURSDAY 8   Cloudy for the most part; at 10 see 2 ships bearing NW from us; they appeared to be frigates, and when nigh to one another hauled up their courses, fired several broadsides at·one another; we put away for them; they separated; we observed they did not fight any more; put about our old course due north. Latitude 29° 51'; night rainy and squally. . . .

SUNDAY 11   Mr. Maly employed in making cot for dog. Mem. Mustered 46 men, officers included, when we left St. Pierre, and 4 dogs; about a week ago lost one dog overboard. Latitude 32° 41'.

MONDAY 12   Fair and pleasant with moderate gales wind; afternoon see three sail bearing WNW; gave chase; at night lost sight of them; they were standing southward; about 10 at night see 1 of them, a brig; at 12 spoke her; from Virginia to St. Eustatius; ordered her to lie to under our lee till morning, it blowing very hard and a heavy sea going. Latitude 32° 12'.

TUESDAY 13   Blustering and a heavy sea; at 1 A.M. it rained very hard; the brig got to windward of us and hove overboard 2 nine-pounders, cannonades, and attempted to run away; we gave her 2 shot; she came under our lee; at 9 Mr. Maly went aboard (the sea running very high); she proved to be as they told us, the *Hibernia*, Captain _____;[9] we told them St. Eustatius was taken February 4th; he said he would go to

9. Those on Waterman's vessel, the schooner *Hibernia*, must initially have thought this brig was trying to trick them by using the same name. Maclay mentions another *Hibernia*, Captain R. Collins (in 1779), from Philadelphia (p. 134). It is possible that this brig is the same privateer, though she seems to hail from Virginia and to be sailing as an armed merchantman rather than a privateer.

St. Thomas [Virgin Islands]; he gave us 4 turkeys.
Latitude 32° 04′. . . .

FRIDAY 16   Light airs of wind and a rough sea; cloudy;
at 9 see a sail; wind died away; out oars; at 3 P.M. the
wind rise; at ¼ past 3 come up with her, the schooner
Betsy from Guadeloupe to Norwich, Connecticut,
William Lathrop, master; been out 22 days; on the 8th
of March she was taken by the *Jamaica,* sloop of war,
from Jamaica to England; she took out of her 9 hogs-
heads of sugar, 10 bags cotton, some coffee, gin, etc.,
and dismissed her, being scant-handed, but would
have plundered her more if she had not made a sail
to windward; the *Jamaica* had 14 6-pounders and 4
4-pounders. . . .

MONDAY 19   Cloudy and cold. . . . At 1 P.M. see Nantucket bearing N by W from us; latitude observed
40° 43′; light rain and distant thunder and lightning.

TUESDAY 20   Cold and stiff breezes of wind; in the morning make Cape Ann; wind blew very hard; got into Portsmouth [New Hampshire] at 7 P.M. . . .

WEDNESDAY 21   At 5 o'clock weighed anchor and went
out of Piscataqua [River]; very cold with brisk gales
wind (NWesterly); got over Newbury bar, but the tide
turning against us, anchored against the fort till 5 P.M.;
then weighed and beat up the river; got as far as the
saltworks; the pilot's boat drifted away; came to anchor;
the pilot got his boat; it being very dark, lay at our moor-
ings all night; very cold.

THURSDAY 22   Fair and pleasant; at sunrise, weighed
and got alongside the wharf. . . .

**IV.   Cruise on the privateer *Fortune*, April 10 to June 28,
1781**

*[Waterman did not stay long on dry land after his cruise to the
West Indies; he did not even go home to Rhode Island. Within*

ten days of his return he signed on with another privateer at Newburyport, and in ten more days he was on his way again.]

SATURDAY MARCH 31, 1781   Fair and cool; agreed with Captain [Joshua] Burgess to go a cruise in the schooner *Fortune* [8 guns, 30 men] for 2½ shares. . . .

TUESDAY APRIL 10   Fair and pleasant; at 9 A.M. sailed in the *Fortune* from the wharf; at 10 A.M. got over the bar; it looking like stormy weather, we put in Sandy Bay [probably Essex Bay].

WEDNESDAY 11   Rainy and high wind from the SE; it like to have drove us ashore; . . . could neither wear nor stay; had much water in our hold; the pump worked very bad; about noon we got into Squam [now Anni-squam]; came alongside the wharf; overhauled her pump and got more ballast in her. . . .

MONDAY 16   Fair and pleasant, the wind nigh N; beat out of Squam; the wind being unfavorable, we put into Piscataqua [River]; about sunset anchored in Pepperell Cove.

TUESDAY 17   Fair and pleasant; went ashore at Dr. N. Todd's; the sailors there capering and tetivating [?]. . . . A new methodical way to teach children—scene: T____d's house; an old woman, sixty; ½ a dozen sailors; 3 young women; 3 or 4 of the old woman's children. After some obscene talk, dinner, several bowls of grog, etc., 1st sailor: "Well, I'll go along. Your servant, ladies and gentlemen. But faith, I must kiss old mother first (smack)." 2nd sailor: "I must have one too; damn my eyes, I'd forgot that (smack)." The old woman grinned as well as 3 or 4 teeth would let her, hugged and wrig-gled up to receive with such a d-mn-bl- grace as put me out of conceit with all women for 4 or 5 minutes at least, one or two others saluting her in the same man-ner. The others declined and shrank by her as if she was a Cheshire cat, ½ devil, grinning, and well they might. The old woman's spirits raised by this as well as the grog drank before, she began to talk and monkey grimace. "I'll tell you how it was last night. I could not go to sleep. Mr. _____ kept hor-hor-hor-hor" (imitating snoring). All her children, etc.: "Hah! ha! ha! hough! ha! hoh! ha!" Then she stood for ¼ hour imitating the snoring; that fund of mirth exhausted, she began upon Mr. W____ H., damning of him, threatening emasculation, etc., etc., etc. Her children thinking it the completest mirth, all joined in chorus for a horselaugh, etc., etc.

WEDNESDAY 18   At 10 A.M. weighed and made sail with a fine breeze and smooth, pleasant weather; went into Casco Bay and anchored about ½ mile from Falmouth [Portland, Maine]. Mem. The snow lay on the ground in many places. . . .

FRIDAY 20   Cloudy and a little rainy; set out to go up the [Presumpscot] River with Capt. Cox [the pilot], but it raining, gave out and came ashore and went to town, coming off in our little flat-bottomed boat with James Smith, John Bryant, Samuel Curry; Smith was skulling and, full of grog and the devil, overset the boat when about 2 rods from the vessel; we all clinched at the boat; she rolled over once or twice; we all got in her again; she, being full of water, sunk right under us; Bryant caught hold of me and sunk me under the water; he let go his hold; we caught hold of the boat again; she rolled over again; Bryant had another clinch upon me and hauled me so far under water that it was a wonder we ever got up again. They called out to them aboard the sloop to swim for the sloop; they all 3 did. I stuck by the boat; she rolled over once or twice till she got bottom upward; I got on her bottom and lay upon my breast; she was so very ticklish, I could but just keep her right, it being very calm and smooth sea; I drifted on her bottom with the tide up the river for about 15 minutes. Mr. Roe hailed a little privateer; they got out their boat; Capt. Burgess and Mr. Bryant being ashore, they pushed off a large canoe and came to me before the privateer's boat; I was chilled so that I could not stand. . . . Thus by the great mercy of God I was saved, it being the greatest chance I ever stood yet by accident. May I never forget this signal favor of heaven, but always remember it with gratitude and trust in Divine Providence.

SATURDAY 21   At meridian [noon] Cape Elizabeth bore west by north, distance 7 leagues; at 7 P.M. spoke the schooner *Rambler* [4 guns, 25 men], Capt. [Joseph] Seveir, from Newburyport, on a cruise. . . .

[The Fortune *sailed in company with the* Rambler.*]*

MONDAY 23   Saw Cape Presu [Fourchu] as soon as light;[1] . . . the *Rambler* informed us that she drove a schooner in Cape Fourchu Harbour; we went in after her. . . . The captain went ashore, his parents living about 4 miles distant.[2] . . . The schooner had a few quintals of fish, a little earthenware, about 80 gals. molasses, and 20 gals. of rum aboard; was going to St. John's [probably Saint John, New Brunswick, rather than St. John's, Newfoundland] for corn; concluded she was not worth sending home. About 9 o'clock at night John O'Brien [not the captain of the *Hibernia*] and John Hall were going ashore; the officers forbid

---

1. Cape Fourchu is the northern peninsula of land forming the harbor of Yarmouth, Nova Scotia. Waterman's spellings (variously Presu, Presew, Bresew, and Bresu) derive from an incorrect understanding of the French name by the first English-speaking settlers. A certificate of proprietorship by the original Committee of New England settlers dated June 15, 1763, refers to Capersu and Capersu Harbour; quoted in John R. Campbell, *History of the County of Yarmouth* (Saint John, New Brunswick: J. and A. McMillan, 1876), p. 41. Here, the place has even lost its identity as a cape. Waterman restored that identity but spelled the name as he heard it. More recently the correct French name has also been restored.

2. Following the expulsion of the Acadians in 1755 and the end of the French and Indian War in 1763, New England frontier seekers began to colonize the coast of Nova Scotia west of Halifax on the south coast and Minas Basin in the north. Tegobue (previously the French town of Thebauque, later renamed Yarmouth by the English), which was established in 1761, was a typical settlement of New Englanders in Nova Scotia. Edward Campbell lists (p. 32) a Joshua Burgess from Connecticut as being an early settler there, who came in the second boatload. Another reference (p. 49) lists both Joshua Sr. and Joshua Jr. It is probable that the captain of the *Fortune* was Joshua Burgess Jr.

them; they persisting in their design, having 2 pistols, and being very groggy, the officers had much ado to keep them aboard; however, it was quelled with broken shins, one forefinger, a jacket tore, and one pistol stock broken.

TUESDAY 24   Cloudy and rainy; in the morning Capt. B. came off; the inhabitants, being mostly settlers from New England, treated him very kindly. . . . At 10 A.M. we weighed and went out the harbor; the *Rambler* had anchored just within the point; the houses appear very thick all along the habor; it is 7 miles up. It continuing cloudy and wind S Easterly, we came to anchor under one of Tusket Islands, being landlocked and fine anchoring ground. . . .

THURSDAY 26   We continued our course [south]eastward in company with the *Rambler;* the wind moderate; at night went in the west passage [between Cape Sable Island and the mainland]; anchored about 3 miles within the point; the *Rambler* went S of Cape Sable; at night the boat went to the settlement on Cape Sable Island; it consists of 4 families. . . .

FRIDAY 27   Fair, warm, and very pleasant; overhauled 2 shallops; . . . they had papers from the British Naval Office, but we dismissed them, taking nothing (but 2 woolen caps, lb. [?] tea, lb. [?] candles, ½ lb. twine); they were bound to Cape Fourchu. At 9 weighed and at noon anchored before the small settlement on Cape [Sable] Island; completed our wood and water, went ashore; the inhabitants have no bread, it being taken by our privateers while freighting from Halifax, etc.

SATURDAY 28   Fair, warm, and pleasant; at 10 A.M. got under way and beat through the passages; up the passage harbor they are settled pretty thick. . . . At anchor about 2 leagues from Point Blanche [since renamed Baccaro Point].

SUNDAY 29   Fair, warm, and very pleasant, with light airs of wind; got under way at 7 A.M.; some foggy; at

4 P.M. came to anchor in Port La Tour; there are a few inhabitants settled in this harbor; they are living very poor, having no bread but potatoes and having no encouragement to fish, salt being 8 dollars per hhd. and fish but 2 dollars per quintal. . . .

TUESDAY MAY 1   Cloudy and foggy; A.M. fair, warm, and very pleasant. The lieutenant and mate of the *Comet,* privateer, Capt. [Richard] Elledge, [of Salem] came on board; the *Comet* was drove ashore at [Cape] LaHave [Island] about a week ago by the *Buckram,* privateer, of Halifax; ten of them got off the island and left ten on; them that got off got 2 shallops and came along shore as far as Cape Negro [Island], from where these 2 came to us, hearing we were here.

WEDNESDAY 2   Fair, warm, and very pleasant; 8 more of the *Comet's* crew came to us in two shallops; we gave them lb. 20 bread, lb. 40 beef, and ½ gal. rum, they intending to pursue their fortune homeward. . . . Came to anchor under the island opposite Cape Negro; boat went ashore and got wood. . . .

FRIDAY 4   At 11 A.M. got under way; the wind brisk at W; standing along the eastern shore; afternoon fair.

SATURDAY 5   At 5 A.M. speak the *Rambler,* a small schooner in company; lay to till 7 A.M. fishing; caught 8 cod; at 8 A.M. see a brigantine bearing NW from us with all the sail she could pack; we then perceiving she was of force, put away before the wind with all the sail we could pack, rowing at the same time for the sand; at 3 P.M. we showed American colors and fired a gun to leeward; she fired a gun to leeward and showed American colors; we fired another gun, at which she took in steering sails, etc., and went by the wind; at ½ past 3 P.M. we put about and went by the wind eastward. . . .

SUNDAY 6   See a schooner coming out Halifax; . . . she made for Ketch Harbour, got in there before [our] boat; we went within a mile of the harbor mouth; saw six sail coming out Halifax; at 1 P.M. put about and stood off. . . .

MONDAY 7   Stretching along eastward; at 10 A.M. see a shallop off Jeddore; at M. bring her to; from Cheda-bucto [since renamed Guysborough] to Halifax, [Captain] Robert Callahan, with 10 moose skins, 400 ducks dead, some quarters of moose almost rotten, some tobacco; we took 2 skins, about 20 fowl, lb. [?] candles, some tobacco. He saw the [schooner] *Resolution* [(6 guns, 25 men) of Boston] and left her to the eastward the 3rd May; informed us that she [the *Resolution*] came alongside an Irish packet in the night and hailed the packet as [if] from Halifax, a privateer, and ordered her boat aboard; her boat came aboard; Capt. Potter got in the boat to go aboard the packet and told his lieutenant to board her as soon as he got aboard; the packet's boatswain overheard it and informed as soon as they got aboard; she immediately fired at the *Resolution* and carried away her foremast; the *Resolution* run off in the night; Capt. [Amos] Potter was sent to Halifax.[3] . . . Dismissed the shallop. . . . We put into Liscomb Harbour; came to anchor about 5 P.M.

TUESDAY 8   Saw 4 sail in the offing; at 9 A.M. get under way and stood after them; they ran into Three Fathom Harbour, where there were 2 more sail; . . . having no pilot, left them and stood for a topsail schooner to windward coming down before the wind; at 10 bring her to; from Canso with hay, [Captain] Thomas Hearty, bound to Halifax; at 11 A.M. Mr. Wescott and Mr. Roe with 8 more went with the schooner and our boat to take the shallops up Three Fathom Harbour; we lay off and on till 7 P.M. and then came to anchor; the wind continues moderate and eastward.

WEDNESDAY 9   Fair and cool; at 6 A.M. weighed and stood toward Three Fathom Harbour; see the schooner

---

3. This story is corroborated in a *Boston Gazette* article dated May 14, 1781, printed in Allen, p. 257.

coming out; at 11 A.M. they came alongside; at M. dismissed the schooner. Mr. Wescott gave the following account of their transactions since they left us, viz.: They went up a creek with the schooner 6 miles till they came to a house where 2 brothers lived and had married 2 sisters [who] informed them that the boats and shallops were 5 miles up the creek, that some neutral French and Indians were settled about the harbor and creek; Mr. Wescott and 5 more went in the boat; they were rowing toward the shallops and saw them stripped of their sails and about 40 cord of wood in a long pile; the people were behind it; they fired at our band; they then concluded to go back, but the British got about 20 in a whale boat and pursued them and landed to cut off their retreat in a narrow part of the creek where the boat must pass, it being pistol shot across, 3 canoes with Indians coming after them at the same time; our people immediately landed and left the boat, took to the woods, and traveled toward the schooner as nigh as they could guess, it being dark; 4 of them got aboard at 11 the same night after traveling about 15 miles; Mr. Wescott and the other got aboard at 6 this morning, very much fatigued. . . . At 4 P.M. got into Jeddore Harbour; came to anchor. . . .

THURSDAY 10   Fair but cool, the wind moderate at eastward; at 8 A.M. weighed and went out Jeddore, beating to windward. . . .

FRIDAY 11   At 4 P.M. came to anchor under the land 6 leagues to westward from Whitehead. . . .

MONDAY 14   Fair weather, fresh gales, wind NNE; at 1 P.M. weighed and proceeded on our cruise; at 6 P.M. anchored in Great Dover Straits [Dover Bay]. . . . Went ashore to search for a cable and anchor hid here last year, taken out of wreck; found they were taken away; weighed and went into the small gut of Canso [at Cape Canso]; anchored above Burying Island. . . .

SATURDAY 19   Cloudy, dirty weather; the crew mutinied,

intending to make the captain return and cruise off Halifax, threatening to go ashore; 3, viz., Bowers, Wheaton, and J. Smith, went ashore; Smith repented and came aboard; the other 2 remained ashore all night. . . .

MONDAY 21   Got under way at 2 P.M.; anchored in Narrowshock [probably Arichat on Isle Madame]. . . . At night we went ashore; fiddled, danced till 11 at night. . . .

WEDNESDAY 23   At 11 A.M. the *Revenge* [8 guns, 40 men], privateer from Salem, Capt. [Benjamin] Knight, came in and anchored; . . . informed us the *Rambler* had taken a Bermudian brig loaded with salt. . . .

THURSDAY 24   At 4 A.M. weighed in company with the *Revenge* and passed through the big gut [Strait] of Canso; there is great plenty of birch both sides the gut and thrifty timber. . . . Came to anchor under the island Louisbourg [Isle Royale, since renamed Cape Breton Island, upon which was the strategic town of Louisbourg]. . . .

SATURDAY 26   At 5 A.M. weighed in order to pass the eastern side of Isle St. Jean [since renamed Prince Edward Island], but finding the passage very full of ice, thought not safe to proceed; altered our course in order to sail between the main and Isle St. Jean. Latitude 46° 02′ N; in company with the *Revenge*. . . .

MONDAY 28   Anchored under the sand [probably on the Nova Scotia coast]; went ashore to get wood and water and ballast; found no good watering place. All along the shore the banks are red stone in stratum, superstratum and red sand; plenty of strawberry vines in blossom, currant bushes, and green grass; the birches were budded, the whole country appearing much thriftier than the southern shore of Nova Scotia; at 10 weighed and stood eastward, the *Revenge* in company; latitude 47° 21′ N; at 1 P.M. it began to blow very hard at SSW; at 3 P.M. beat in under Cape Tormentine and came to anchor, the *Revenge* in company; it continued to blow very hard all night. . . .

WEDNESDAY 30 [At] anchor under Cape Tormentine, the water appearing very red, also all the banks on shore; in some old draughts it is called the Red Sea, as well it may. We conclude to go back and cruise off Halifax. Went ashore; got wood and water, greens; the land appeared thriftier than any I have seen yet; plenty of strawberry vines in blossom, green pea vines in great plenty; the trees were larger than any I had seen on any part of this coast; consist of black and white birch, oak, maple, ash, beech, fir, spruce, and pine; saw where the Indians had made a fire and roasted fish, fowl, and cockles; the sea had washed up plenty of dulse and some sponge; there is plenty of sarsaparilla and sassafras; 'tis said no codfish are caught in the Bay of Fundy and western side of [Isle] St. Jean, the water being reddish and muddy. . . .

THURSDAY 31 At 9 A.M. saw a sail bearing ENE; light airs wind; all hands to oars; at 11 A.M. brought her to, a shallop belonging to Tatamagouche; 2 men [who] by their looks were shocking poor were in her, French Germans from Lorraine; were very poor; the shallop was small and nothing but ballast; they had freighted some seal oil for the Indians to Charlottetown on [Isle] St. Jean; we took a small anchor and cable, a gun, a sealskin knapsack, compass from her and dismissed her and made sail. . . .

FRIDAY JUNE 1 Finally settled our minds to go back and cruise off Halifax; before this the design was as variable as the winds. . . . Beat toward Canso.

SATURDAY 2 Got through the big gut Canso; . . . came to anchor before Narrowshock; went ashore and had a dance.

SUNDAY 3 Weighed and beat out Narrowshock; at 11 A.M. brought to a shallop from Halifax bound to Narrowshock; we took from her a basket of birds' eggs, lb.

25 small rigging, a small pot; she belonged to old Thomas Jacquet Delouer; when we first came to Narrowshock, he came aboard and showed his permit from the General Court of Massachusetts, his protection from Chevalier [Admiral] Ternay, and the French consul at Boston; thinking himself out of danger, he slyly told us that some of his neighbors had no permission and had 2 shallops which would be a good prize to us; we did not meddle with them; he now fell in a trap he set for his neighbors. At 1 P.M. we came to anchor in Canso, where lay the brigantine *Tiger* of 14 4-pounders and brigantine *Bloodhound* of 12 3's and 4's [both of Salem]; last Monday they took in company a large brigantine and ship from Antigua bound to Halifax; the ship had 500 hhds. rum, sugar, and molasses; the brigt. had 150 hhds. of ditto aboard and 200 cases of gin; the captain of the brigt. and 2 more were wounded; the *Tiger* had 3 wounded; Mr. Darby that was drove ashore in the *Comet* was aboard the *Tiger*. . . . At night old Delouer came down from Narrowshock in high passion, intending to go to Boston for satisfaction, saying further that Capt. B took from his a silk handkerchief, cloth for a shirt, 1 pair of trousers.

MONDAY 4   The wind increased to a violent gale; our anchors not being sufficient to hold, our schooner drove, as luck would have it, against the head of Mr. Peart's fish stage; had she missed that, she must inevitably have stove against the rocks; she got so nigh shore at low water, she was fast aground, her bottom lying on the sand, all hands wishing for her to stave to pieces so that they might go aboard the *Tiger*. The *Bloodhound* did but just escape going ashore; surf ran very high. . . .

WEDNESDAY 6   At 8 A.M. weighed anchor with an intent to go out, seeing a brigantine in the offing; the *Bloodhound* weighing at the same time, got their anchor fast to our cable; she had like to have gone ashore; we cut our cable and freed her, got out our boat, and dragged our grappling; found the cable and anchor and immediately put out the harbor; the [wind] blowing hard. Meantime, the *Bloodhound* put out after the brigt. and soon disappeared, and the *Tiger*, in getting under way, had like to have drove ashore; she out anchors again, and we left her and stretched away westward; the wind blowing very fresh; we came to anchor under the land in a cove much like Tarpaulin Cove, where we lay all night.

THURSDAY 7   At 2 P.M. came to anchor in Liscomb Harbour. . . .

SATURDAY 9   Thick, dark weather with a fresh gale at eastward with heavy rain; at 3 P.M. the wind shifts to SW, blowing very hard; . . . continued rainy and foggy through the night; finished every drop of rum aboard. N.B. Have 26 men on board; there are 7 languages understood among us, viz., English, Dutch, Irish, French, Spanish, Latin, Indian. . . .

MONDAY 11   At 1 P.M. saw a schooner and a shallop; the schooner was too fast for us; the shallop ran among the islands; at 5 P.M. gave over chase and went into Fishermans Harbour and anchored; the wind blowing very fresh; went ashore, caught great plenty of lobsters; clams very plenty.

TUESDAY 12   Weighed in order to put to sea; saw a large ship in the offing; supposed her to be a cruiser beating to westward; returned in harbor; caught great plenty of lobsters. . . . Nine weeks today since we left Newburyport. . . .

SUNDAY 17   At 9 A.M. saw a schooner; soon after saw another schooner with a brigantine in chase; . . . the brigt. and schooner join; gave chase to the first schooner we saw; finding by their signals they were Americans, went into [Beaver] Harbour, where found the brigt. to be the *Hibernia* [10 guns, 60 men], Capt.

Jeremiah O'Brien.[4] . . . All of us anchored in company. . . .

THURSDAY 21   We saw 3 shallops going in Little Harbour; we put in there again; they were from Narrowshock, being some families of men, women, and little children, about 20 in all, with their household goods aboard and cattle, about 16, being very poor; getting grass for their cattle and food for themselves by the way, having nothing but potatoes to eat. Duces putaverunt capere duo shallops pro nobis. Dixerunt idem eis; illi lacrymaverant dolentes nam res hae fuerunt totum ut habent et movent nunc ubi inveniant meliorem locum habitare. Nos duces tacti fuerunt in corde a paupertate sua et relentant.[5]

FRIDAY 22   Saw a sail stretching along eastward; . . . [it] was the schooner *Rambler,* Capt. Benjamin Fuller;[6] came in [Little] Harbour; had plenty of butter, sheep, hogs, and calves aboard he had taken from some Malagash [since renamed Lunenburg] shallops; we concluded to send home the best shallops. . . .

[The Fortune *sailed in company with the* Rambler.*]*

WEDNESDAY 27   At daylight Halifax Lighthouse bore WNW; saw a large brig going in the harbor; sent the whale boat; found her to be a merchantman; we gave

---

4. This brigantine seems to be a different *Hibernia* from the schooner Waterman sailed in under Jeremiah's brother John O'Brien in the West Indies. Jeremiah had squeezed a lot into the period since about March or April when he was still incarcerated in the *Jersey* prison ship. In three months or less he had been transferred to Mill Prison, Plymouth, England, escaped from there to France, returned home, and, taking command of this *Hibernia,* sailed to the Nova Scotia coast. See notes 1 and 4 of part III above.

5. Translation: "The officers planned to take two shallops for us. They told them this; they cried sadly, for these things were all they had, and they were now moving them in order to find a better place to live. Our officers were touched to the heart by their poverty and relented."

6. This is the same *Rambler* (4 guns, 25 men) which the *Fortune* last heard was in Nova Scotia waters before May 23, under the command of Joseph Seveir. Whether during the intervening month the *Rambler* returned to Newburyport and sailed again with a different captain or whether a change in command was made at sea for some undisclosed reason is not clear. Fuller had previously commanded the *Rambler* late in 1780. See Allen, p. 249.

chase with both schooners and whale boat; the wind light; out oars; we chased her till she got as far as Chebucto Head; saw Halifax town; finding it in vain, gave over chase and stood windward; our shallop continued her course westward and quit us. . . . About 4 P.M. saw a ship and brig coming out Halifax in chase of us; wc out oars, beat and rowed; the wind at N Westward, a moderate breeze; we went between the lighthouse and main; the ship and brig continued beating to windward without the lighthouse till dark, when we lost sight of them and made the best of our way for Pennant Bay, where we anchored in company.

THURSDAY 28   Our provisions being nighly expended, concluded to go home with all possible expedition; Capt. Fuller of the *Rambler* wanting me to come aboard and the captain and all the officers [of the *Fortune*] consenting, I accordingly went in the *Rambler,* leaving the *Fortune* about 11 A.M., having been aboard 79 days, 4 of our hands leaving at the same time. . . .

V.   Cruise on the privateer *Rambler*, June 28 to August 8, 1781

[This being for Waterman a continuation of the same cruise, though now on a different privateer, the diary continues with the same day he changed ships.]

[THURSDAY JUNE 28, cont.]   Weighed and put out of [Pennant] harbor; cruising off the mouth of the harbor. . . .

SATURDAY 30   At 4 P.M. dispatched Mr. Howland and 9 men with Mr. Whalen, one of the prisoners, in the boat to take [Halifax] Lighthouse; at the same time, got under way to go there also; beat out the mouth of the harbor; it coming on thick with fog, we returned at 5 P.M., but the boat proceeded. . . .

SUNDAY JULY 1   At 3 P.M. got under way and went out;

a very large swell setting in from the southward; met the boat returning from the lighthouse; she captured the lighthouse and left 4 men there and brought off 9 muskets, 6 lb. powder, about lb. 250 lead, some musket balls, etc.; at 6 P.M. came to anchor in Pennant harbor. . . .

TUESDAY 3   At 4 A.M. dispatched Mr. Howland and 4 men for the lighthouse; at 11 A.M. weighed and stood out Pennant harbor; came to anchor at the mouth of the harbor. . . . At 2 P.M. Mr. Howland returned with our men and the things captured from the lighthouse, viz., 1 bbl. flour, 1 bbl. pork, 2 spyglasses, 2 large iron chains, 1 12-pound gun, 1 ladle, 1 copper lamp, 1 compass, 10 gals. molasses, 12 lb. sugar, 1 bbl. cider, 2 powder horns, 2 shallop's sails, 2 boat's ditto, ½ bbl. tar, 1 iron pot, 2 tierces, and 1 bbl. oil, two boat rodes, etc. . . .

WEDNESDAY 4   At 5 P.M. got into Dover[1] and came to alongside the fish stage, not long since occupied but was plundered last year by an American privateer of 4 hundred quintals of fish; the house and fishhouse remain yet with something of a garden, etc. . . . At 1 P.M. saw 2 sail in the offing; dispatched Mr. Howland and 4 men in the whale boat after one and Mr. Hicks and 2 men in the long boat after the other; at 3 P.M. Mr. Hicks came up with his chase, fired 1 musket, brought her to; a shallop from Malagash bound to Halifax with shingles. Mr. Howland came up with his at 4 P.M., fired 4 muskets, brought her to; a shallop from Chester bound to Halifax with shingles, some butter; he saw another boat in the offing steering west; he brought her to; from Port La Tour bound to Halifax with eggs, butter; at 5 P.M. saw another sail in the offing steering westward, bearing SW from us; Mr. Hicks went to him,

1. Modern maps distinguish East Dover and West Dover, just a few miles to the north and west of Pennant Bay. One should not confuse this place, as Waterman did (July 7), with Little Dover on Dover Bay near Canso, far to the northeastward of their present position.

with 3 men taking care of the last prize, and Mr. Howland went for the other; at 11 P.M. came up with her; a shallop from Malagash for Halifax with hay, potatoes, salmon, eggs, and butter, an old woman, and 2 small boys. All the prizes but the last came into Dover and swung at the schooner's stern, who lay at anchor all night; 2 women were passengers and one Capt. Britain, an old acquaintance of Capt. Fuller.

THURSDAY 5   At 4 A.M. Mr. Howland got in; at 8 A.M. his prize got in; the old woman fell to lamenting and begging; the shallop was too leaky to send home; we took out salmon, butter, and eggs and dismissed her with the others at 11 A.M., except the first that Mr. Howland took; at 10 dispatched Mr. Wills and 1 hand in the whale boat for home laden with king's stores taken at the lighthouse and 68 salmon; at the same time, Mr. Jackson and one more for home in the shallop first taken by Mr. Hd. for home laden with shingles. . . .

FRIDAY 6   Mem. Yesterday, as the Malagash shallop with hay was coming alongside, the old woman set to bellowing and crying at such a rate (for fear her shallop would be taken) that most of our people began to rejoice, thinking they had a Malagash calf aboard, till they came alongside, and then they found their mistake. . . .

SATURDAY 7   Saw a schooner; supposed her to be the observer of mouth of the harbor; at 6 we weighed and rowed in a small creek, where we came to alongside a rock, being landlocked every way from the main passage up the harbor, having high rock cover with spruce around us; at 8 A.M. our boat went out, saw the schooner beating up the harbor; we began to secure our provisions in case our vessel's taken; the schooner we saw at the entrance of the harbor came to anchor in Little Dover [sic] and sent her boat among the islands in search of us; as we observed from the rocks and hills, they did not discover the least of us; hauled down our schooner to clean; the mosquitoes, flies very tormenting. . . .

MONDAY 9   At 8 P.M. Mr. Howland, myself, and six more set out upon a cruise in the shallop *Katy* [a prize]; we got off Prospect Point and lay to there. . . .

TUESDAY 10   The shallop saw a whale boat in Pennant harbor; at 10 A.M. took her; she had 7 bbl. salt and 130 fathom [of rope] for a rode; we unloaded her and dismissed her; we got back to the schooner at 4 P.M.; while we were gone Mr Crawley and 3 more came aboard; they were drove ashore in a schooner, prize to the *Resolution,* loaded with dry goods, taken in the Bay de Chaleur; the *Resolution* took a sloop there full of furs and dry goods, also a brigantine and another schooner; these people came from Canso in a birch canoe; some shallops fired at them nigh Devil's Island. 13 weeks from home.

WEDNESDAY 11   Yesterday Mr. Hicks and 7 men set out on a cruise in the *Katy;* he saw a sail in the offing; found her to be a privateer; she chased him; at noon he came back to us, the privateer in chase. . . . The privateer attempting to come in to us, we landed 2 parties of men, both sides the creek, leaving a small party aboard the schooner, and held ourselves in readiness to engage them. At 2 P.M. she opened around the point of land upon us; hailed her thrice; received little or no answer; fired a broadside and a volley of small arms at her; she wore short around upon her keel and came to anchor and hoisted American colors; hailed him again; answered from Salem and hailed us; we informed him who we were; sent his boat ashore; Mr. Howland went aboard; the schooner *Hawk* of 8 gun, Capt. Cornelius Thompson, from Salem [soon to be Waterman's captain]; he came aboard us. Presently we saw 11 sail to the westward stretching eastward; we rowed out, the wind being small, and stood after them in company; night coming on, we lost sight of them but stood eastward all night.

THURSDAY 12   At 7 P.M. Mr. Howland, myself, and 8

men set out on a cruise in the *Katy*; . . . stretched along eastward; at midnight were between the lighthouse and main.

FRIDAY 13   We came under Devil's Island [possibly McNabs Island?]; at anchor 3½ A.M. . . . We lay the SEasterly side of the island; had a view of the passage up the town [Halifax?]; saw the blockhouse and a ship at anchor. . . . We lay under the island till 9 A.M. when a shallop passed us and gave her chase; took her; the first escaped; we ran for another; took her; . . . we brought all under D.'s Island; they had little aboard; . . . dismissed [one] shallop with prisoners; they stood for Halifax, we southward, putting two men in each shallop and 4 in the *Katy*. . . . Standing SWestward all night in company.

SATURDAY 14   At 6 P.M. speak the *Rambler* at the mouth of Pennant Bay. _____ Faxton, George Bailey, and Sam Curry went in the *Katy*; William Fleet (who we took the 29 June, who joined us) and James _____ went in one shallop, the gunner and another in the other shallop, Mr. Hicks and 2 men in the schooner; all orders to go to Dover; it came on foggy and variable winds all night; lost sight of one another.

SUNDAY 15   We found ourselves in St. Margarets Bay; we stood along shore till we came into Dover in the NWestern straits. . . .

MONDAY 16   At 7 A.M. dispatched Mr. A. Crawley and _____ Parker in the prize schooner for Newburyport. . . . We saw a sloop of Prospect steering W; we supposed they got intelligence of us and had hemmed us in, several shallops being in company with the sloop; we took out all our provisions and ammunition, etc., and hid them in the woods and hid our boat loaded with stores around the point in a very low place; we watch their motions; the sloop and schooner continued their course westward; one of the shallops was seen with the gunner's [shallop]; he informed us the sloop spoke with him, was the *Fox* [8 guns, 40 men], Capt. [Levi] Doane, from Boston; we got all our affairs aboard and re-mained at anchor all night.

TUESDAY 17   At 11 A.M. two men . . . came aboard and brought James _____ to us, the man we put aboard the shallop with William Fleet; he informed that Fleet, when in Pennant [Bay], asked James to give him a spell at the helm; then he went and loaded both muskets and put them and many other things in the canoe and told James he was going to leave us and says, "Tell Capt. Fuller I have stayed with him long enough," after which James ran the shallop ashore at Prospect, where he was kindly entertained and brought to us; they offering to get off the shallop for us, we gave them a bbl. flour, etc. We dispatched the shallop with Mr. Jackson and Mr. Johnson (one of the men that was drove ashore at Canso) for Newburyport. . . .

WEDNESDAY 18   At 9 A.M. saw a large brigantine about 1½ leagues from us, the E side of Shad [Bay] and north of Betty [Island]. She lay hid among the islands; being landlocked, we altered our course and stood westward; she immediately made sail and stood after us; the wind SW, moderate breeze; we ran for [St.] Margarets Bay; she gains upon us; we ran in among the islands the E side the bay and ran the *Rambler* ashore about 40 rods S of Hosier River about noon. We landed what we could, ammunition, provisions, etc.; hid our boat; I got all my things aboard except a matrass [?]; hid my chest in the woods; our boatswain (Robert Kelly) having got angry a few day ago, we left him at the vessel, and fear-ing he would join them, myself, Pettingill, and another went after him; could not find him. . . . [The British] came across the boat, gave a huzza, and fired a volley of small arms; this was about 1½ P.M. I took my pack, pistol and marched back where the captain and most of our men were; found a cutlass some of them left in the woods; took it; came up with Mr. Hicks; he had just found two men in the woods with a gun, ax, and dog; they were laborers; had been out in the woods building a canoe; they told us they had a hut about 1 ½ mile from us to the northward; they were afraid the brigt. people would find their hut, rob it; I went with one of their men for the hut; crossed Hosier River; found James _____ at the side of the shore; he had been firing at the schooner; we went down to the shore; saw them getting off the schooner; heard them talk, the marines firing a volley in the woods often. I proceeded with the stranger for his hut; came across several remains of Indian huts and gardens; he informed that the Indians were gone for Halifax to confess to the priests (they being Roman Catholics), and they expected them back soon, Indian Phillip being their chief, who is hired by government [at Halifax] to take up deserters, Americans, etc. We at last came to their hut, it being by the side of the water; they had lime, kiln burnt, and expected a shallop from Halifax every day to take in the lime; they had some smoked salmon, some maidenhair [fern] tea ready made; I took a drink and salmon and found all safe there and came off; saw the brigt. [and] poor old *Rambler* beating out; the brigt. was yellow-sided, a very fine one to look at; she had 12 guns and very many men aboard; when they first came to the schooner, Mr. Hanscom fired at them, having them in fair view; saw them put one man in the boat; heard several cry out; he that commanded the [brigantine] saw one of our men and says, "You damned rebel rascals, I have a good mind to fire at you (and took up a gun). I have a good mind to let you all perish ashore here; but you may tell your captain, if he'll come here, I will take him aboard." He was not answered. At night 14 of us collected together; we could not find the captain, Samuel Willard, the boatswain, and William Stoneman; we lodged under the trees; did not make us a hut; the 2 strangers with us; the mosquitoes, flies very thick.

THURSDAY 19   These 24 hours begin with fair, pleasant weather, attended by thousands of mosquitoes. Got up early in the morning; went down to the place where the schooner was drove ashore; collected our things together; they did not find our powder; they rolled a bbl. of bread in the water, found Mr. Howland's chest, broke it open, and hauled out the things and carried off most of them; we found one pistol of theirs on the shore that was broke at the muzzle. I went with one of the strangers (a Scotsman; the other was born in Nova Scotia) to their hut; drank tea there; went a mile further northward to look out if any boats were along shore; saw nothing; brought 4 salmon; came back at 5 A.M. Mr. Howland, Mr. Hicks, J. Hall, and Mr. Hanscom set out for Prospect to get our shallop [the one run ashore last Sunday by James _____]; we built a hut with spruce and fir boughs; kept a watch through the night and a fire. . . .

FRIDAY 20   These 24 hours begin with fair, pleasant, but hot weather. At 11 A.M. Samuel Willard and William Stoneman returned to us; they had been lost in the woods ever since they were drove ashore; they went off with Capt. Fuller; he soon got out of sight of them; they wandered till they got entirely lost; were in such a hurry to run away, they hove away their packs, provisions, and guns; had a pistol with them and made fire; were very hungry; they got 2 young birds yesterday and a frog last night and one small clam today; when they came in, were miserably bit with flies and tore with bushes. N.B. They meant to give themselves up prisoners; had lost all other hope; prayed, cried, and read Mary Rowlandson.[2] Johnson, one of our men, in going

---

2. Although reading might seem a strange companion with praying and crying while lost in the woods, this is apparently what Waterman meant to say. Mary Rowlandson, according to the *Dictionary of American Biography*, was an inhabitant of Lancaster, Massachusetts, when, during King Philip's War, on February 10, 1676, "the Indians attacked Lancaster, burnt the village, and carried away captive Mrs. Rowlandson and her three surviving children." One child died; after a long ordeal Mrs. Rowlandson and the other two finally were ransomed for £20 on May 2. Soon after, she wrote a book about her experience entitled *The Sovereignty & Goodness of God, Together with the Faithfulness of His Promises Displayed, Being a Narrative of the Captivity and Restauration of Mrs. Mary Rowlandson*, which was first published at Cambridge in 1682. It is this book, apparently a "best seller" for some time, which it seems Willard and Stoneman were reading while lost in the woods, when they themselves had good reason to fear capture by Indians.

in the woods, got lost; we fired several guns, but he did not return.

SATURDAY 21   These 24 hours begin with fair weather and very hot; Johnson returned in the morn; at noon saw two canoes with Indians coming in the bay; knowing their treacherous disposition and expecting more soon, we concluded to up duds and travel for Dover and Prospect; we got all our powder and guns with most of our provisions and traveled southward, sometimes through bushes and sometimes by marshes, about 4 or 5 miles; going around a cove, we saw a shallop; concluded it was Mr. Hicks in search of us; fired a gun; they answered the same, luffed to, and beat in for us; at 6 P.M. she got alongside the shore; . . . she had been at our encampment and, not finding us there, came along shore for us. They informed us they went from our camp to Dover, swam on the island, hailed a shallop (bound for the lime making nigh our camp); she came to, took them in; they went to Prospect; found Capt. Fuller there (he got there in 10 hours); they left him and Mr. Howland there to bring the shallop run ashore there last Sunday; we built a fire on the shore and lodged under the trees.

SUNDAY 22   At 9 A.M. got aboard the shallop; got under way and went to our old encampment; got the remainder of our things; went to the strangers' hut; got a relish of smoked salmon; they gave us salmon and bread; at 11 A.M. put off again; saw our shallop with Capt. Fuller aboard coming in. N.B. The Prospect people informed Mr. Hicks yesterday that the brigt. had 2 men killed and 1 wounded when she drove the *Rambler* ashore. At noon speak Capt. Fuller and Mr. Howland; they found great difficulty in getting the shallop; the former owners, hearing she was at Prospect, sent 2 men who took possession of her and had carried her sails in the woods; they by force got her from them, together with some meat and bread aboard. Ten guineas was bid for Capt. Fuller and £5 per man for the others at Halifax. . . . At 5 P.M. got alongside the stage [at Dover] with all our hands together that were drove ashore (except the boatswain, Robert Kelly; we concluded he went aboard the brigt.), 17 in number. . . .

[They discharged the shallop going to the lime kiln and prepared the one Captain Fuller and Mr. Howland had recaptured to carry them back homeward.]

We called this shallop the *Rambler* and entered into articles similar to those aboard the old *Rambler.* . . .

MONDAY 23   Cast off from the stage and put to sea, beating westward; the wind SSW, a good breeze. . . . N.B. Our shallop being open except 2 cabins in the fore cuddy, we got plank at the fish stage and laid a loose deck. At 7 P.M. came to anchor under an island off Malagash; we divided all our provisions, having about lb. [?] salmon, lb. [?] bread, lb. 2 pork, and about lb. 1 codfish apiece. . . .

TUESDAY 24   At 4½ A.M. weighed anchor and continued our course westward, beating along shore. . . . At noon Malagash bore N from us; at 2 P.M. saw a shallop west of us close in shore; stood no chance to take her; . . . at 6 P.M. came alongside the fish stage at False LaHave; only one family living here (——— Jenkins), but found nobody here at present except 2 dogs and a calf. . . . At 7½ P.M. cast off from the stage and anchored between [Cape LaHave] Island and main; the mosquitoes very thick and spiteful.

WEDNESDAY 25   These 24 hours begin with thousands of tormenting mosquitoes and foggy weather and a moderate breeze; old Jenkins not returning and we being distressed for provisions, took the calf and a few fish drying and a couple pieces of pork; at 6 got under way and stood westward. . . .

FRIDAY 27   Saw a whale boat; at 7 A.M. speak her, a fishing boat with 2 very poor men aboard; we borrowed their boat to go ashore to get provisions, . . . we being about 1 league E of Ragged Island. . . .

SATURDAY 28   At 5 P.M. came to alongside the rocks at Cape Negro Island, the N side; wooded and watered; went ashore and got plenty of gooseberries, there being also strawberries, raspberries, green peas, etc.; at 10 A.M. cast off and came to anchor little way from shore; foggy.

SUNDAY 29   At 6 A.M. weighed and went up the western harbor [near Baccaro Point]; at one _____ Greenwood's, got 27 dried salmon, and now having provisions to carry us across the Bay of Fundy, and completed our water to 70 gallons, at 9 A.M. got under way and stood S to clear Cape Sable. . . .

MONDAY 30   Very foggy; at 11 A.M. see a schooner to windward; her course NW, the wind northerly; she had a head of two topsails and forestaysail; the fog being very thick to lee, she did not see us, or if she did, she did not notice us; we saw but only the man at helm with spyglass; at first sight she was within musket shot; we bore away and soon lost sight of her. . . .

TUESDAY 31   At 4 A.M. out oars; at 6 A.M. a moderate breeze spring up SWesterly; heard thunder at a distance; 16 weeks from home. . . .

WEDNESDAY AUGUST 1   Calm at 5 P.M.; out oars; at 6 P.M. spring up a gentle NEaster; at 8 P.M. calm, out oars again; having but one bbl. water, came to allowance of 3 pints a man per diem; rowed till 11 P.M., when sprung up a small breeze of wind NE; course NW by W; very pleasant evening. . . .

FRIDAY 3   A good breeze at ESE; course NW by W; away before it wing and wing; set a blanket for a water sail. At 10 A.M. saw a sail off deck bearing from us NNW. She gave us chase; we went close haul upon the wind; at noon saw land bearing NNE; the sail gained upon us fast; at 3 P.M. spring up a brisk gale; we keep ahead of the chase till 5 P.M., speak her; a schooner-shallop from Salem on a cruise for the coast of Nova Scotia, Capt. Peter Martin. We requested water and bread of him; he gave us (after some delay) about 3 pints water and 3 biscuit per man and nothing more; we quit him and steer W by N. . . .

SATURDAY 4   At 4 A.M. in with the land; at 6 A.M. went in a small cove ¼ mile N of Cape Elizabeth; got breakfast ashore; got water and ½ bushel meal; at 9 A.M. cast off from side the rocks and make sail for Falmouth. . . . At 2 P.M. get alongside the wharf. . . .

SUNDAY 5   A moderate breeze at SE; cast off from the wharf and beat out the harbor. . . . At 6 P.M. Cape Elizabeth bore W. . . .

TUESDAY 7   Got against the fort [at Newburyport] by midnight.

WEDNESDAY 8   At 2 A.M. got alongside the wharf, having been gone 120 days.

VI.   Two cruises on the privateer *Chace*, September 13 to December 22, 1781

[Waterman remained in Newburyport for almost a month. Early in September he traveled to Salem, where he signed for another privateer cruise.]

WEDNESDAY SEPTEMBER 5, 1781   Fair and hot; got over to Salem; agreed to go out in the brigantine *Chace*, Captain [Cornelius] Thompson. . . .

THURSDAY 13   At 11 A.M. went on board the *Chace*, brigantine of 10 guns, viz., 3 sixes, 4 fours, and 3 threes; at 1 P.M. weighed and stretched up and down the channel; at 4 came to anchor in the channel a mile below the town. . . .

FRIDAY 14   At 11 A.M. got under way and stood out the harbor; the wind SW; at 6 P.M. Cape Ann bearing SW by S, 3 leagues distant; we steer NEastward. . . .

MONDAY 17   At 8 A.M. saw a brigt. northward of us; . . . she bore down upon us; we put away before the wind; find we gain fast from her; shorten sail for her to come up with us; at 3 P.M. she came pretty nigh us; we fired a gun under American colors; she fired a gun, but we could not see her colors distinctly; she lay to for us; she appeared to be a brigt. of force and endeavoring to get under our lee; we put away from her; she fired a gun at us; the shot went over us; she out all sails and put after us, but we soon leave her. Latitude 43° 01′ observed; we steer NEastward.

TUESDAY 18   At noon saw the land bearing N of us; we haul our wind and steer along shore eastward; latitude observed 43° 45′. At 5 P.M. see a small sailboat go in a harbor; we go in; it is called Port Mouton, is a little westward of Liverpool [Nova Scotia]. At 6 P.M. see 2 small schooners coming westward within [Mouton] Island that makes the harbor; . . . at 8 P.M., it being dark, they come nigh to us; hail them; a privateer schooner [*Thrasher* (8 guns, 30 men)] (Captain [Benjamin] Cole) from Salem and her prize. . . .

WEDNESDAY 19   See a topsail schooner pass the harbor to the eastward; . . . at 1 P.M. weighed and ran out the harbor between the island and main; the schooner we saw pass us got out of sight, going in some harbor, but we continue our course eastward (Capt. Cole returned to Port Mouton). The wind blowing fresh westward.

THURSDAY 20   In the night saw the light at Cape Sambro Lighthouse; made short sail; at 8 A.M. lay to to fish; caught plenty of cod. . . .

FRIDAY 21   At 1 P.M. came to anchor in Little Dover [*sic;* see note 1 of part V above]; remain at anchor all night.

SATURDAY 22   Employed in shortening the foremast about 30 inches. . . . At 2 P.M. see a large sloop close hauled upon the wind, stretching in for Halifax; we made all the dispatch possible; at ½ past 3 got under way, but she got very nigh within the lighthouse and fired several guns; we saw at the same time a sloop SE from us and a brig SSW; we give the latter chase; she made from us, the sloop for us; night coming on, the wind freshens; we stand NE by E under full sail all night.

SUNDAY 23   The wind increasing; beat into Owls Head and came to anchor there at 4 P.M. . . .

MONDAY 24   At 2 weighed and stood out the harbor; saw two small shallops standing eastward along shore; at 4 bring them to; they were from Halifax bound to Chedabucto, being inhabitants of the last mentioned place; had a few barrels provisions aboard for winter stores, being poor people; we gave them victuals and drink and dismissed them and came to anchor where we did last night.

TUESDAY 25   At 11 A.M. get under way; see a small sail stretching along shore westward; when they saw us they made for us; at noon spoke them; a shallop from Louisbourg bound to Halifax, having a few bricks, an old man, and 2 boys; appeared to be very poor; said they had been 5 weeks from Louisbourg; . . . they aboard the shallop had nothing to eat but fish; we gave them bread and meat and dismissed them. . . . Remain at anchor in Owls Head.

WEDNESDAY 26   It coming on foggy, we go into Jeddore Harbour and moor; caught plenty lobsters, it being sandy bottom; remain at anchor in Jeddore. . . .

FRIDAY 28   At 8 A.M. see a brig putting out to sea; we stand for her; at 11 A.M. speak her; fired several shot before she would strike; she gave us three shot; was the *Lady Hammond,* Capt. Ellis, bound to Nevis [British West Indies] with lumber, etc.; had 11 men and 6 3-pounders.

SATURDAY 29   Stand southward with our prize; [at] noon left her, she standing SWestward; we put Mr. _____, prize master, and 5 hands and 2 prisoners [on her]. We standing northward, the wind moderate at northward.

SUNDAY 30   At 9 A.M. see a ship within shore of us; at

the same time saw the lighthouse bearing NNE of us; we give chase to the ship; gain fast upon her. . . . At 3 P.M. we come up with the ship; engage her; we keep under her stern; she could bring no guns to bear upon us; she fired several shot at us but to no effect; we fired 8 guns at her; she struck; she was a prize to the *Chatham*, a 50 gun; was taken four days ago off Cape Ann; was in a set of ballast; had 10 six-pounders and 14 British and 2 American prisoners aboard; we sent Mr. Silver, our lieutenant, and 6 men aboard and left her to give chase to a sloop we saw coming down upon us; just before we took her, a hawk come aboard us and caught a sparrow that had taken refuge aboard us; we chase the sloop till she put away from us SE by the wind; we go down to our prize and take out 9 prisoners and stand SSW. . . .

[After a relatively short cruise of one month, with only one prize but with several British prisoners on board, the Chace *sailed homeward toward Salem.]*

SATURDAY OCTOBER 6   At 5 A.M. saw Cape Ann bearing SWesterly; saw a brigt. the southward of us; she gave us chase; we stood by the wind with larboard tacks aboard till off Ipswich Bay and then tacked and stood along shore for Cape Ann Lighthouse. At 4 P.M. came to anchor in the channel 1 mile below the town [of Salem]; went up to town in a boat.

SUNDAY 7   Mem. Our brigt. we took got in last Friday night. . . .

[After a two-week wait in the Salem area, Waterman sailed again on the same privateer with the same captain.]

SUNDAY 21   Fair and warm; at 11 A.M. weighed and put to sea in the brigantine *Chace* on a cruise; the wind brisk at NW; only 26 men and boys aboard and 1 dog.

MONDAY 22   Cold and a stiff breeze at NNW; in the morning off Casco Bay; at noon came in the harbor of

New Meadows [River, just west of Cape Small, Maine]; saw a small shallop-schooner that came to anchor at the mouth of the harbor; ... we weighed and stood out for her; she did not run away; she was from Cape Fourchu [Nova Scotia]; had 80 quintal dry fish on board; they had a bill of sale from the former owner at Yarmouth (nigh Cape Fourchu); ordered her to follow us in the harbor of New Meadows, where we came to anchor; at 4 P.M. the captain went on shore and tarried all night, it being his native place. ...

THURSDAY 25　At 6 P.M. got under way and put to sea; the wind NW, a good breeze; stood for Penobscot Bay all night.

FRIDAY 26　At 8 A.M. off the bay; put in; saw a sloop and a schooner; gave the schooner chase; she rowed, and the wind being small, she got through an inlet in the NE part of the bay; we beat in among the islands in the N part and came to anchor.

SATURDAY 27　At 8 A.M. bring to a small schooner with fish and lumber from Union River bound to the westward; we dismissed her; ... at 5 P.M. came to under an island southward of our former station. ...

TUESDAY 30　The inhabitants bring off milk, mutton, and vegetables to us; N.B. This island is called Holt.

WEDNESDAY 31　At 8 A.M. got under way and beat up the harbor; at 1 P.M. came to under Butter Island; Mr. _____ Annis reigns sole lord and emperor here, he having first settled here about 3 years ago; has a small spot of land cleared. ...

THURSDAY NOVEMBER 1　Saw a schooner coming out of Bagaduce [since renamed Castine; a British stronghold]; we got under way immediately and stood for her; at 7 P.M. speak her; a flag of truce bound for Boston, having the crew of the *Amsterdam,* Capt. McGee, a letter of marque taken by the *Allegiance,* coming from Europe for Boston; she was worth £24,000 sterling; we beat back.

FRIDAY 2   These 24 hours begin with rain; at 1 A.M. came to under an island; the wind came on to blow very hard at NE; it continued rainy through the day; remain at anchor. . . .

[For several days the storm raged.]

TUESDAY 6   The weather moderates; the wind fresh at NNW with flying clouds. . . .

THURSDAY 8   At 2 P.M. get under way and stood eastward; at 5 P.M. came to in the northern part of Eggemoggin Reach [east of Deer Isle]; the wind increasing cold.

FRIDAY 9   It snowed about an inch deep; remain at anchor.

SATURDAY 10   At 4 P.M. got under way and stood southward; at 5 P.M. came to in Benjamin River [in Eggemoggin Reach]. . . .

[For several days the Chace *remained in this area, during which time no prospective prizes came its way.]*

FRIDAY 16   At 9 A.M. got under way and stood out Penobscot Bay; fine, pleasant weather; going at the rate of 4 or 5 knots; smooth sea; our course ESE, intending for Cape Fourchu. . . .

SUNDAY 18   Cloudy, dirty weather, the wind at E by N, veering to northward and increasing to blow; continue our course WNW; came to under Matinicus Island [off the Maine coast] in a small cove almost surrounded by rocks; continues to rain and blow throughout the day. . . .

[With continuing stormy weather, the Chace *made but slow progress toward the Nova Scotia coast.]*

FRIDAY 23   The same weather as yesterday; at M. see the land bearing N; we being in latitude by observation

44° 16′, conclude the land to be Cape Sambro; the wind hauling to WSW, we stand in for the land; at 2 P.M. ship a sea that ran in great plenty in our cabin; at 6 P.M. make Jeddore; at 8 P.M. anchored in the same; the wind somewhat moderated.

SATURDAY 24   Saw a sail off the mouth of the harbor; get under way immediately, the chase standing westward; at 11 A.M. come up with chase in Owls Head harbor; she was a schooner (the *Rachel*), a British transport cut out by American prisoners last night; they were 12 in number; had cut out the spikes out of a large, thick lower port of the prison ship [at Halifax] with a small, 2-bladed penknife and puttied up the holes days; they then brought over a sentinel (a Spaniard) belonging to the refugees [loyalists], Emanuel Dixon; he, refusing money, agreed to assist them away for the sake of liberty; they knowing when it was his turn to stand at the poop (the boat made fast to the stern), he hauled her up and put 2 oars aboard; 11 men got in; they could persuade no more to go off; he then hollered out "all is well" and slid down on the painter and then cut her away. Immediately one of their oars broke; they paddled and rowed aboard a schooner; found nothing in her, no ballast nor any people aboard; they left her, taking out a spyglass and musket and got aboard the *Rachel;* as they cut away, they heard musket fire aboard the guard ship; they first stood westward; the wind being against them and carrying away their maintopmast and having no water aboard, they stood eastward. About a fortnight ago [before this escape on the *Rachel*], 2 Americans (of the aforesaid 11), Capt. Smith and Mr. Bradish, got aboard the boat [of the prison ship] at noonday and put ashore; the guard fired at them as soon as they put off but did not hit them; they made out to get ashore but were headed [off] by 2 soldiers and brought aboard and put in irons till day before yesterday. They inform that the Americans are treated very ill and die fast, having the smallpox among them. . . .

SUNDAY 25   At 3 P.M. got under way and stood up the western harbor Owls Head and came to anchor; the schooner [*Rachel*] got under way at the same time and anchored not far from us. . . .

TUESDAY 27   Cold, blustering, but fair weather and wind NW and continues so through the day; the schooner drove ashore SWestward from us.

WEDNESDAY 28   The *Rachel* being ashore and having one small poor anchor, the Americans conclude to burn her and set her on fire. . . .

THURSDAY 29   The *Rachel* continues burning through the day; remain at anchor. On a point of land in this harbor, 4 Englishmen were burnt by the Indians; the stake to which they were tied remained there a few years past. . . .

FRIDAY 30   Mem. All the Americans come aboard us together with the British, viz., 11 Americans, 1 Spaniard, 6 British, 36 of our own crew, total 54. Remain at anchor.

SATURDAY DECEMBER 1   Put out to sea, standing westward along shore. . . . At 2 P.M. see a large ship; gave her chase; at 6 come nigh her (she being within the [Halifax] Lighthouse); she gave us 4 stern chasers (supposed 3-lb. cannon); we get pretty nigh her; saw 13 ports of a side; hailed her; she answered from England, the *Robust;* she being so nigh Chebucto Head, we thought fit to quit her, there being many British ships in Halifax that could easily put out to retake her. We stand westward for Dover. . . .

SUNDAY 2   At 9 A.M. see 2 sail standing westward; we get under way and give chase; at 2 P.M. came up with the hind one, a shallop from Halifax bound for Rossway [at the head of St. Mary's Bay]; ordered her in for False LaHave, where we came to anchor. . . .

MONDAY 3   At 11 A.M. we saw a brigantine; . . . we gave chase; . . . at 3 P.M. hail the brigt.; from Antigua

[British West Indies] bound to Halifax, David Ross, master; been out 48 days; had 7 men and 1 passenger aboard, about 40 hhds. rum cargo; man her and take out all [men] except the passenger; stand southward. . . . At 11 P.M. see ship stretching eastward; we in shore of her; ordered the brigt. [prize] to stand eastward; the ship passed us without molestation though within gun shot; she stood for the prize; we tack and stand for her to draw her attention from the brigt.; she stood her course. About 1 A.M. the prize's boat came alongside of us with all our people in her, they having left the prize with only the passenger aboard, the ship being very nigh her; at the solicitation of the captain, they returned to see if the ship took possession of the brigt. or no.

TUESDAY 4　We standing for the ship till 2 A.M.; then tacked and stood westward, firing a 4-pounder; stood our course till 6 A.M.; then came to anchor in Port Mouton bay; at 7 A.M. the boat returned with all our people in her, they having no chance for the prize, the ship taking possession of her. . . .

WEDNESDAY 5　Remain at anchor in Port Mouton.

THURSDAY 6　Dismissed Mr. D. Ross and 5 men (an Italian and American remain with us), also the mate and 3 men of the *Rachel,* giving them paroles and the brigt.'s long boat. . . .

SUNDAY 9　At 3 P.M. get under way and stand eastward; the wind light at NNW; at 4 see a sail bearing E of us; she was stretching in shore; we could not perceive what she was but supposed her to be a ship or brigt.; . . . at 6 P.M. see her again; hail her (she appearing like a brigt.); answered us "from sea"; hailed her name; answered "the *Atlanta*"; we stand off a little; lost sight of her; at 9 P.M. she was within land of us and musket shot off; she hailed us and [we] asked "what schooner?" (we doubting she was a brigt.); she not understanding us, hailed again and again, giving out some threatenings; we found our mistake and, convinced it was the *Atlanta*, stand off WSW, the wind veering around to the eastward.

MONDAY 10   Continue stretching along westward; at 9 A.M. make Cape Sable on our starboard bow; the wind increasing to blow very fast; we make for Shag Harbour and came to anchor about 1 P.M. . . .

THURSDAY 13   At 9 A.M. weighed and stood westward within Tousquet [Tusket] Island and at 10 A.M. came to anchor in Argyle Bay [east of Tusket Island], a very fine one, being landlocked; the weather squally, wind WNW attended with some snow; an American came on board who escaped Halifax. . . . At night the [crew] go ashore and take geese and hogs from the inhabitants, unknown to the officers. . . .

SATURDAY 15   At 9 A.M. we come to anchor the westward of Argyle; last night some of the people wanting to go ashore to plunder the inhabitants, the captain forbid them going and hoisted the boat aboard; they attempted to hoist her out but, being detected, threatened very high that they would have the boat. This morning the captain was informed that several threatened to carry the brigt. in another port; called them up and put them in irons. . . . At M. see a shallop stretching in from the westward; at 2 P.M. bring her to; from Salem, a smuggler belonging to Solomon Rider of Argyle. . . .[1]

SUNDAY 16   Agree with S. Rider to ransom the shallop for 700 dollars; settled the affair and dismissed her; remain at anchor; very cold.

MONDAY 17   At 6 P.M., the wind springing up a moderate breeze at NEastward and looking like good weather, we get under way and put out, intending for New England shore. . . .

---

1. This shallop was evidently smuggling goods from Salem into Nova Scotia via Argyle for use by local inhabitants or possibly by British forces.

TUESDAY 18   At 9 A.M. make Mount Desert [Island, Maine] on our starboard bow; continue stretching along WNW; at 11 A.M. make Penobscot islands; our deck clogged with ice. . . .

WEDNESDAY 19   We put into Townsend [Thomaston ?] harbor and at 10 A.M. came to; dismiss 7 of our hands who belong to New Meadows and also 4 men who came out of Halifax prison [ship]; at 12 A.M. get under way and put out. . . .

FRIDAY 21   Stand along shore for Salem; at sunset Cape Elizabeth bore WNW; very cold; the wind continues brisk, NW.

SATURDAY 22   At 1 A.M. off Cape Ann; the wind veering around southward; beat in Salem harbor and at 11 A.M. come to anchor off the fort. . . .

[Waterman remained to celebrate the anniversary of St. John the Evangelist on December 27 with members of the Masonic lodge at Salem. From there he traveled to Newburyport, then via Ipswich to Boston, where he arrived on January 1, 1782. The diary ends on January 5 without further significant entries.]

GLOSSARY

cartel . . . . an agreement between belligerents for the exchange of prisoners of war; in this case, the vessel used to convey the prisoners being exchanged

drogher . . . . . . a sailing barge used in the West Indian coastal trade

dulse . . . . a coarse red seaweed

gill . . . . a glassful amounting to one-quarter pint

rasher . . . . a slice of meat

rode .... a light rope for a boat's anchor

shallop .... a small open boat, usually without a deck, used chiefly in shallow waters

sling .... a drink made with one of several types of liquor plus water, sugar, and sometimes bitters

vendue .... an auction

Types of seagoing vessels, as distinguished by their rigging:

ship .... three-masted, square-rigged vessel

brig .... two-masted, square-rigged vessel

brigantine .... variation of a brig, with a fore-and-aft-rigged mainmast

schooner ..... two-masted, fore-and-aft-rigged vessel

sloop .... single-masted, fore-and-aft-rigged vessel, sometimes with a square-rigged topsail

Types of naval vessels (which were mostly rigged as ships), as distinguished by the number of guns:

ship of the line .... 60 to 100 guns

frigate and small two-decker .... 20 to 56 guns

sloop of war .... 8 to 18 guns